MW01709891

# Balanced Dog

Learn to Cure

**Any**

Dog Misbehavior

By

**Bruce Warrington**

ISBN 978-0-9959100-0-3 (print)
ISBN 978-0-9959100-1-0 (eBook)


Cover photos: mikeblackphotoworks.com



For information: www.canadiandogwhisperer.ca

First edition published in Canada

# Contents

# Part Two

## Dog Park Lessons

## ***Preface***

As a dog whisperer my goal is to teach dog owners *the canine way*, to think like their dog and win at what I call the Game of Canine.

I consider dogs to be black or white animals. They are either leaders (black) or followers (white), with no other options. To your domesticated dog, the pack is the whole family and each family member is considered either a leader or follower. As descendants of wolves, this is deeply rooted in their DNA.

Humans are more nuanced or gray because we can discuss or negotiate with each other through logic and our ability to reason.

The trick is to play their game, the Game of Canine, with *black or white* in mind, and diligently follow the eighteen rules to posture your dog as a follower. Do that, and you can become an incredibly effective *master* of the game. If, however, you are not consistent or do not play by the rules, you don't have a chance of victory. It is us humans that must conform to the *canine system.*

Dogs and humans have the same two expectations of each other; for the other to speak their language, and for the other to know what they want. We speak English (or any other language), and they speak Canine. We think they speak our language; otherwise, why would we continuously talk to them, expecting them to understand? They will never adapt and speak English, so we must make the adjustment and learn the language of canine.

When you *win* at the Game of Canine, you'll have a balanced pack with contented, subservient, obedient dogs. The result? A happy combo-pack: people and dogs.

## **About the Author**

It is not often that one gets the opportunity to turn their hobby into a career and a business. I have been an entrepreneur from about age ten (paper boy, lawn maintenance and snow clearing on my street, as well as an upscale Kool-Aid stand on the golf course near my home). I started my first business at age twenty-one and have been involved in owning/operating businesses ever since.

I've been a dog aficionado all my life. I love training dogs, reading about dogs and generally anything to do with dogs. In 2004 I discovered *dog psychology* and was hooked. I read books of every published dog behaviorist that I could find available online, in every library and book store; in fact, I read them over and over to ensure that I effectively absorbed everything that I possibly could. The sole purpose of my study was for my own pleasure, to learn more and more about how dogs think. To be able to see through the *eyes of a dog* deeply touched a natural cord of curiosity in me.

At the time, I had no plan whatsoever to turn my new knowledge into a business; in fact, I had never considered my love for dogs from a business perspective. Then I met Dan, a wealthy business man, who told me about his misbehaving dog, Nike, a Schnauzer/Poodle mix, who barked incessantly at the doorbell, nipped the kids, pulled on the leash and was aggressive toward other dogs while on a walk. Dan had developed a major dislike towards Nike and considered him his wife's dog. I explained that dogs have no concept of ownership; all members of the family are part of the pack.

With my help Nike became well behaved in short order. As Dan paid me he said, "I would have paid you multiples of what you charged. I can't believe what you accomplished in one evening." My years of in-depth study suddenly became reality as I, for the first time, applied my knowledge for a fee. For Dan and his family, I wrote a curriculum that unknowingly would evolve into the Game of Canine.

Soon afterwards I began helping other families with their *problem* dogs. Next, I made some business cards, and in no time, I was a part-time *dog whisperer*. Within six months I was dog whispering full time. And as the saying goes, "The rest is history." To date I have worked with over 1,500 dogs and fortunately I can say that I have yet to meet a dog that cannot be balanced; simply because I do things their way.

The key to curing dog misbehavior is through re-aligning the pecking order, so that humans land on the top and canines land on the bottom, of the hypothetical *Leader Ladder*. Many of these misbehaving canines and their owners will be mentioned throughout the book. Each dog I work with teaches me something and enhances my awareness of the *canine way*. It's a joy to witness the transformation, as stressed families with misbehaving dogs become the happy balanced combo-packs, dogs and humans, that every family yearn for. I cannot express how incredibly rewarding this is for me. My insatiable desire to broaden my knowledge and awareness about canine behavior presses me to continue learning and develop new techniques to pass on to dog owners.

## Introduction

The mandate of this book is to teach dog owners like you the *canine way*; how dogs think and how to balance your dog. Balance means the hierarchy of your pack is clearly in order and your dog looks up to you as being higher on the totem pole, or *Leader Ladder,* as I call it. A balanced dog will respect, obey, serve and trust you as *leader of the pack, or alpha.* An unbalanced dog develops misbehaviors, disrespect and lack of trust. The constant throughout this book is to help you think like a dog. *Everything* is from the canine point of view.

The positive result of a healthy balanced pack is being able to *control the calm.* This means that you can put your dog in a calm mode anytime, anywhere and in any situation. When this takes place within five seconds of your command, your dog is in balance and implicitly showing you respect.

I teach dog psychology like a game. I call it the *Game of Canine.* This game may be new to you, but it is certainly not new to your dog. Thanks to their canine DNA, dogs are masters of the *game.* This book will teach you *their* rules and how you can become a master yourself, climbing the ranks on your Leader Ladder, (see Chapter 6: The Game of Canine, for a full explanation).

There are eighteen rules in the Game of Canine. Once you know all the rules to *their* game, you can win the game at will. Even children can master the Game of Canine if they follow the eighteen simple rules.

Throughout this book I will introduce you to multiple concepts of dog psychology that are core to dealing with all dogs, balanced or unbalanced. This book facilitates an incredibly simple and effective system designed to yield a balanced pack within your home. And as I said, a pack includes dogs and all family members.

I've created a fictitious teacher named Brewster, who on Sunday mornings volunteers at a local leash-free dog park and teaches a new lesson weekly to visitors on how to cure specific misbehaviors of their dogs. At the end of these lessons you will be familiar with many reformed, well behaved dogs.

Each dog-park chapter also includes a true *dog whisperer* story; something I have experienced in my practice that relates to the chapter lesson. At the end of each chapter you'll find a summary outlining the chapter lesson, which can act as a future quick reference for a specific misbehavior.

# Part 1

# The Game of Canine

## Chapter 1

## Three Relationships to Create a *Balanced Pack*:

*Dog Whisperer; Dogs; Dog Owners.*

For me to balance a family pack I must first work with the dog(s) to balance them; then the dog owners to teach them how to retain their dog(s) in a balanced mode; it is then the owners' job to follow the rules to the Game of Canine for a lifetime of happiness.

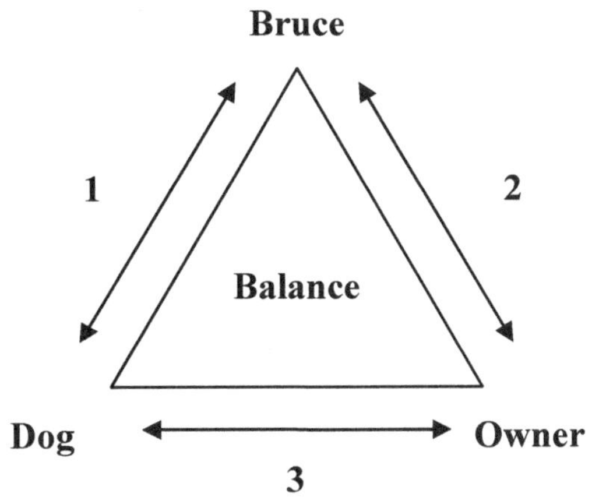


**Relationship 1: Dog and me.**

When I arrive at a client's home, I immediately take-over-the-pack, from the canine point of view. The dog must recognize me as the new leader of the pack and accept being relegated to the follower/submissive role. I become the new *king of the castle*. This usually takes only a few minutes or sometimes a few seconds, because dogs are reactors. They don't have the ability to reason and process things like us. They simply react to whatever is presented to them.

I call this process *balancing* a dog. From their perspective, I am 100 per cent top dog, alpha or leader of the pack. They become zero leader and therefore 100 percent follower. Once a dog is in balance, they tend to relax and accept the realignment of the pecking order or hierarchy. This is the *canine law of nature*. All inconsistency and confusion are eliminated.

Balancing is a very calm, quiet process. There is no yelling or aggression from me in any way. In fact, I never talk to the dogs I work with. I talk to their owners to explain the process, as most people do not notice or realize what is transpiring. As subtle as the process appears to us humans, it is very distinct to our pets.

The first thing that I do is put a slip lead on a dog as I enter the home. This connects us and gives me control, which is especially needed if they become aggressive. I also make strong eye contact. There is no blinking, they must be the first to blink or look away. Next, I take their space by very slowly stepping closer and closer, possibly touching them at this point, to move them backward and give up their space. This would certainly be considered rude human behavior, but it is confident, strong, dominant, canine behavior.

Their options are to either accept me as the new *alpha* or fight me for the position. Fortunately, most dogs accept their new subservient position without much ado. But not always.

**Relationship 2: Dog owner and me.**

As a dog whisperer, my relationship with a dog owner is a process of education. My mandate is to educate owners in *the canine way*: how dogs think; the relevance and intricacy of the pack hierarchy; how to maintain the new hierarchy realignment; how dogs communicate and ways to communicate with them; the simplicity and significance of filling the role of leader of the pack; ways to interrupt negative behavior; and to be more proactive in canine management.

Dog behavior is a mirror reflection of owner behavior. Therefore, owner behavior is the cause of dog misbehavior and must be altered to change a dog's behavior. As a dog whisperer, I teach Dog Psychology 101. Humans must learn the canine *modus operandi* – stop trying to humanize their dogs and start seeing the world through *their* eyes. When humans *get it* and practice living the canine way, dogs are naturally content in a follower's role.

Once you, as a dog owner, learn and practice the eighteen rules to the Game of Canine, you will be able to maintain a balanced dog forever. You will be able to control and calm your dog anytime, anywhere and in any situation, in less than five seconds. The rules to the Game of Canine are innate to all canines – it's their DNA. I don't teach dogs anything. They know exactly how to be a dog. There are two opponents in the Game of Canine; dogs and humans. It's not a fair matchup because dogs know all the rules to the game and dog owners know only some. This gives a dog a major advantage. But once dog owners learn all the rules, it is they who have a distinct advantage, because humans are smarter and can beat dogs at their own game. (See Chapter 7: Eighteen Rules to the Game of Canine, a.k.a. *The Recipe*).

**Relationship 3: Dog owner and their dog.**

When dog owners learn and implement all the rules to the Game of Canine, they can retain the new realignment of the pack hierarchy. This invokes a balanced relationship between owner and dog, from both the dog's and the owner's perspective. If the dog does not view you as his leader, then you are not. The core of the Game of Canine is; *control the calm to win the game*. When an owner controls the calm, he or she scores points. If a dog controls the excitement, he scores points. A military general must be in control of his troops 100 percent of the time; dog owners must emulate this ranking theory within their own pack. It is natural for our four-legged best friends to understand this system of ranking.

There are only leaders or followers, one or the other, with no in between. It's either black or white. The alpha/leader's two very distinctive roles are to dominate and to protect the pack. The follower's specific roles are to; respect, obey and serve the leader. Followers revere the leader like a god. Humans, on the other hand, are *inconsistent gray*. This is not the canine black or white way, where there must be no melding of job descriptions.

Dogs know how to live with dogs, as humans do with humans. Problems arise when humans and dogs live together. Neither tends to see things from the other's point of view. Oddly, we expect dogs to speak our language and understand our ways; just as dogs expect us to speak their language and act in a canine fashion. Because it is impossible for them to understand our point of view, it is we, the humans, who must adjust and start seeing the world through their eyes.

Throughout the book I frequently repeat the following paragraph:

**My biggest hurdle when teaching dog psychology is getting *gray* humans to act like *black or white* canines. This is not because it is complex or difficult to understand; a child can follow the rules. It's inherently unnatural for us to act *black or white* – our DNA is *gray*.**

We are much more complex due to our ability to reason. The only black or white of humans is that we are either alive or not, and women are either pregnant or not. Humans must focus and diligently practice these new rules. If you follow a recipe to bake your favorite cake, it turns out the same every time. If you accurately follow the rules to the Game of Canine, or *The Recipe*, you will achieve and maintain a balanced pack forever.

Pack balance is a very special experience. I am extremely fortunate to live with a balanced dog. His name is Satchmo, his nickname is Louis Armstrong.

## Chapter 2

## Dog Whispering Versus Dog Training

*I teach humans the 'canine way'.*

**Dog whispering** is a psychological process that deals with a dog from a mental viewpoint. Understanding the canine mind gives a dog whisperer the insight to change negative behavior into positive behavior. The key is to know why a dog does what he does and connect with them – their way.

I never talk, nor whisper, to the dogs that I work with.

**Dog training** has been around since wolves and humans bonded some 10,000+ years ago and is an absolute necessity when raising a dog. Training a dog to understand various commands is a repetitive process that must also include a reward system for good behavior, often known as positive reinforcement, which can be with a verbal praise, touch/petting, a treat or a favorite toy.

Early obedience training for puppies can help prevent the development of future misbehavior. While taking obedience classes, people often have specific, focused training sessions one or two times per day. As a dog owner, it's important to monitor your pet's behavior and condition during longer sessions. Don't overload your dog, especially in hot weather. Always end each session on a positive note.

I suggest that you augment these regular training sessions utilizing any combination of; come, sit, stay, down and heel commands – many times throughout the day. You can also add any other commands as you see fit. I'm often asked, "How many commands per day should I give my dog?" There is no set number because each dog is different. I suggest that you aim for twenty-five commands per day, focusing on; come, sit, stay.

These short, frequent repetitive training commands over the course of the day will accelerate the learning process. This is prudent when working on realigning your pack balance. In one week this would add up to 175 commands and in four weeks the grand total would be 700 commands. These short bursts of commands are given over and above regular longer training sessions. The result of this is dramatic in terms of pack realignment.

Some dogs thrive on training and love to work, while others not so much. I know that Satchmo loves it, and he gets dozens of orders or commands every day. For example; every time he goes out of or into the house, he sits and waits for me to tell him it's OK; it's the same when he goes in and out of the car. He heels while walking; sits and waits at the edge of the park until I call him; waits at the bottom or top of stairs as I go up or down (I don't want to get bowled over and break my neck); sits and waits when visitors arrive . . . the list goes on and on, throughout each day.

If you want an obedient dog, you must give them the attention that is required (practice makes perfect). This also develops a strong bond between dogs and owners. I believe the louder you yell, the bigger the echo. The bigger the effort that we put into something, the bigger the return. Training a dog can be an extremely rewarding hobby.

Consistency is the key ingredient to this process. Human inconsistency is a major cause of canine behavioral problems, as dogs cannot respectfully follow a leader who exhibits instability. Everything must be considered from a dog's point of view. It is irrelevant what we humans think. If a dog perceives you to be in the leader position, then you are; if not, you're not. I often ask dog owners; "If you asked your dog to point to the leader or leaders of your pack, whom would she likely point to?" Most owners say the dog would point to them, but the reality is that most dogs would likely point to themselves, or at least include themselves in the leader category. This results in a serious maligning of the pecking order, from the dog's perspective. The fact that she thinks of herself to be in the leader category, even sometimes, is a defining issue.

There are many tremendously effective ways to train dogs, just as there are many ways to get to the center of town. Some methods are quite passive and *nurture* a dog to learn a specific behavior. This typically involves the frequent use of treats whenever the dog completes the command given, to encourage repetition of the behavior. Treats will accelerate the learning process and are used by almost all dog-training schools. I, however, believe the prerequisite to giving treats is a touch and verbal praise. This should be the primary form of reward, while treats are secondary. If you don't have a treat with you, you can always give a verbal praise and/or a touch.

Other training techniques involve using more physical methods; e.g., choke collars, slip leads, prong collars or electronic collars. Each of these collars has a place in controlling a dog's negative behavior when more passive methods are ineffective. I consider these collars to be an assertive/positive technique when accompanied by positive reinforcement, touch and/or treats.

This more physical style of dog training is designed to 'correct' negative behavior. When used properly, these collars do not cause pain; they simulate a nip or bite in the neck area. If you watch dogs play or rough-house with each other, you'll see them nip and bite each other in the neck area, at the top of the neck or throat. This mild form of aggression is not meant to hurt the other dog, but it can sure sound aggressive – like they are killing each other.

Passive trainers typically refute these tools, or any assertive methods, because of the physical factor. A passive trainer would also consider grabbing a dog by the scruff of the neck as a negative method of training. I certainly respect the views of both passive and positive/assertive training methods. The main objective of assertive/positive techniques is to simply shock the dog; not hurt the dog. It's like someone lightly poking you in the ribs. You jump because you are shocked but not hurt. To shock without hurting is the objective. Anything that produces positive results must be considered successful, if a dog is never hurt in any way.

Note: Police dogs, military dogs and guard dogs are all trained to be aggressive and bite when necessary. Therefore, the methods used for these dogs are a lot more forceful than those taught in a typical dog-training school. But these trainers too, would never hurt a dog. Because these working dogs are very strong-willed and naturally forceful, they need strong, assertive training to be effective in getting the results mandated. Passive training would be totally ineffective, as the mission is to develop these dogs' prey-drive and get them riled up in preparation for being aggressive with bad guys.

Because dogs are descended from wolves, we should be able to learn about the canine mind by studying wolf behavior.

Wolves/canines are always direct; there is no discussion or tolerance whatsoever. Canines are unable to be *gray* to negotiate or make idle threats. Their threats are always very serious (often described as vicious); there is no confusion, their meaning is deadly clear. I consider a wolf to be playful, loving and *soft* animal within the pack on a regular basis. But I also know they can be very aggressive when differences develop. A wolf fighting over a position in the pack is not uncommon; it can also be fatal. Their aggression is part of their DNA, especially when killing for food to survive or when defending their pack or territory.

We humans can also be extremely aggressive and sometimes lethal. During hockey games, fights break out regularly, and this is considered part-of-the-game. We watch cage fighting, boxing, football – even soccer and basketball can be aggressive. An Olympic judo match, for example, is obviously physical and aggressive. As humans we are both passive and physically aggressive with each other. We are the only animal who can compassionately negotiate, yet instantly become physically aggressive towards each other. I believe that we are the only animal that kills each other for reasons other than as a food source or protecting ourselves.

Like humans, dogs tend to deal with each other in both a passive and aggressive way. When interacting with their owners or each other, their physical aggression can result in a bite, preceded by some passive form of a warning that humans often don't recognize or pay attention to.

The methods that I use when dealing with dogs are both passive/positive and physical/assertive/positive. Dogs respond extremely well to my calm, strong energy, along with some simple body language. If I need to give the leash a correctional light pop to interrupt and get their attention, this is part of the physical way in which I deal with canines. I also use my leg to nudge them, which unbalances them enough to redirect their focus. Sometimes I put my hand on the back of their neck, exerting a slight downward pressure, or even hold onto the scruff of the neck with my fingers. This is certainly physical/assertive/positive but would not be considered aggressive. I always add a positive praise and/or touch when negative behavior changes to positive behavior.

The most significant physical action is to pin them down or lift their front feet off the ground, by either pushing down on their neck or pulling them up by the scruff. This only happens if they are showing aggression (snarling, biting) or if they were totally insubordinate and wouldn't cooperate. I use this method as a last resort but with no anger, no malice or hurting them in any way.

I do not hesitate to briefly hold a puppy down or lift him off the ground by the scruff when he is being a brat, just as his mother did mere weeks before he was adopted and entered the human world. A mother dog will grab her pup by the back of the neck and growl if he is being impish and disrespectful toward her. Dogs, as well as raccoons, cats, lions and a plethora of other animals, carry their young by the scruff of the neck. This is physical/assertive, but *it does not hurt*; it is a natural process for many species, which is why I simulate this physical behavior with dogs. Again, a positive praise and/or touch should follow a positive change of behavior.

Over the years, I have viewed many videos about wolves. Once I watched a mother wolf teaching her one-year-old pups to fish. The river beside them was abundant with salmon swimming up river. Three of the four pups were feeding with exuberance. The fourth was not participating in any way, only watching from the sidelines. The mother, using her mouth, grabbed him by the scruff and pinned him down while growling at him. She didn't hurt him, but she was certainly very physical/assertive and vocal. As soon as she released him, he walked into the river and grabbed a salmon to eat. Lesson learned, with no anger, no malice, no pain and no holding a grudge by their mother; like humans often do. Also, she never takes *no* for an answer.

Note: I recently watched a litter of six-week-old pups who were in the process of being weaned. Three pups approached their mother to suckle her. She growled and snarled, with a raised lip to indicate she was having no part of it. They immediately turned and paraded off toward their litter mates. One of them decided to try again. The mother grabbed him by the scruff with her mouth, pushed his head to the ground and let out a much bigger snarl and growl – then let him up. He, very nonchalantly, walked off to be with his siblings with a wagging tail. He wasn't upset in any way.

In my work I typically deal with a wide range of misbehaving dogs and sometimes extremely aggressive dogs. I have had tremendous success using a combination of both passive/positive and physical/assertive/positive training methods.

I have never hurt a dog in my life, other than accidentally stepping on a tail or foot. My mandate when dealing with dogs is to mimic canines without the aggression or pain that they often exhibit to each other.

Typical dog misbehavior consists of: jumping; uncontrollable exuberance; nipping; biting; separation anxiety; soiling; being destructive; fear aggression; nervousness or insecurity; aggression to humans or dogs; pulling on the leash; guarding; barking; won't listen, or won't come when called; digging; doorbell aggression and general dominant behavior when a dog thinks that he's *king of the castle*. All the above behaviors can appear in combination and can vary from mild to extreme.

# Chapter 3

## Canines: Wolves and Dogs

*Look different; act the same.*

It is said that the DNA of all domesticated dogs is about 98 percent to that of a gray wolf. In North America there are hundreds of domestic breeds. Man created each breed for a specific purpose, e.g., to assist him in hunting, for protection, herding, companionship etc. The list is lengthy. I know that it is hard to conceive that a Yorkshire Terrier or Bassett Hound are descended from a wild gray wolf; it is much easier to imagine the German Shepherd Dog, Siberian Husky or Malamute. Yet they are all descendants of the gray wolf.

We can learn how the domesticated dog thinks by studying the ways of the gray wolf. By understanding his pack mindset and dealing with our dogs from a canine point of view, rather than a human point of view, we can learn how to live with our pets in harmony and balance. (Canines include wolves, dingoes, coyotes, foxes, feral dogs, domesticated dogs and many others.)

Every canine pack has a definitive ranking within the hierarchy, consisting of leaders and followers. The hierarchy, or pecking order of the pack, is extremely important on a canine's mind. In a wild pack, the *alpha pair*, a male and female would be No. 1 and No. 2 in the pack. Often a pack has only one alpha, either the male or female. If the alpha male is killed off, then the female instantly becomes No. 1 and rules the pack herself, until she accepts a male as a new co-alpha leader, with whom she will breed. Typically, the alpha pair are the only pack members to breed.

The followers in the pack have a fundamental job; to respect, obey and serve the leaders. The followers align themselves in a very distinct pecking order, starting with the *beta*, who is the No. 1 follower. He is the most likely candidate to challenge the alpha, likely his father, for future leadership. The lowest member of the pack is the *omega*, who is treated with such an inordinate amount of disrespect that we would consider it cruel or torturous. All other followers fall somewhere in between the beta and omega in a very distinct order of ranking. This pure canine hierarchical system is the epitome of *survival of the fittest*.

The alpha leader(s) has two very specific jobs while running the pack:

**1. Dominate the pack**

It is his/her job to keep order within the pack and decide when and where they will go hunting, change living locales, as well as anything else that needs to be dealt with. The alpha leader will emphatically carry out these responsibilities, as the survival of the pack depends on every member following the rules to the nth degree. If a pack member does not obey the alpha's command, they would be dealt with in an aggressive, physical way. An alpha will surely attack the disobeying pack member, as he *never takes no for an answer*.

The leader of a pack is constantly on-duty, whether sensing for danger or making decisions for the pack. Being a pack animal, he/she always acts in the best interest of the pack and never in a self-serving way. Alphas eat first to maintain their strength; this ultimately ensures the safety of the pack, as well as their food supply. The alpha is the main decision maker, rather like a general in the military.

**2. Protect the pack**

It is his/her job to protect the pack from intruders, such as other wolves, cougars, bears etc. The leader would not necessarily be the only one to fight. Options to protect against intruders include: freezing and letting the potential danger move on without detecting the pack; fighting to protect the safety of the pack; or taking flight, the whole pack can run away from or go around the potential danger, but this would be an executive decision made only by the alpha.

Another component of the leader's job is to sometimes leave the pack on their own while he checks out their territory. While away the alpha would be looking for signs of other wolves marking in their territory, tracks of other animals to be assessed as either a food source or a danger, potential new living accommodations, as well as a water supply.

# Chapter 4

## Two Common Dog Owner Mistakes

*Nobody's perfect.*

**1. Forfeiting the leader's position.**

In the wild canine world, the pack cannot survive without having a leader 100 percent of the time. If the alpha is killed, the job is immediately filled by either the alpha bitch or the beta, the No. 1 follower. A leaderless pack would result in anarchy, with no one to rule. This would result in fighting within the pack.

From the dog's point of view, when humans step out of the leader's role, metaphorically speaking, a dog is obligated, by the law of canine nature, to fill the role. As we continuously oscillate in and out of the alpha role, unbeknownst to us, our behavior results in major canine confusion.

If a dog thinks *he* is the leader, then *he* must dominate and protect his pack. When we don't like his dominant, protective behavior, we then take back the job. However, soon afterwards we give up the role, again forcing the dog to reassume the leader position. This back and forth, or flip-flopping, is the major cause of canine misbehavior and understandably so.

The canine mind perceives this inconsistent leadership to be unstable, weak and not conducive of a balanced pack, which creates the exact misbehavior that we don't like. This is a *self-inflicted* curse of many dog owners. When the confusion is replaced by clarity and consistent leadership, the negative behavior will dissipate, but not until then. Confusion is the root cause of almost all misbehavior.

Here is a human comparison: Imagine my friend Rick and I are going for a ride in the car. I say, "I'll drive," and off we go. About two blocks into the ride I say to Rick, "I don't want to drive any more, you drive now." He takes the wheel and very shortly after I say, "I want to drive now." We again change seats and I take over. After another short distance I say to Rick, "I don't want to drive anymore." This back and forth of me changing my mind causes tension and confusion between Rick and me; no wonder.

**2. Saying to your dog, "You are the leader, not me."**

Many, many times every day we say to our dogs, "You are the leader, not me." We don't say this in words, we say it through our actions. If we said it in words, there would be no negative ramifications because dogs don't speak English. Because most of us don't speak the language of *canine*, we can easily convey this message to our dogs without knowing what we've 'said'.

By consistently changing this message to, "I am the leader, not you," we can clarify and clear up a myriad of confusions and therefore eliminate most of a dog's negative behavior, (for a complete list of how to show leadership through our actions, see Chapter 30; "Six Ways To Say I'm The Leader, Not You."). To send a clear message, we must think like a canine. Almost all dogs are happier in the role of follower. When leadership is clear, they are much more likely to respect, obey, and serve their great leader.

## **Three Gears**

Dogs have three gears: forward, reverse and neutral. Our obligation as dog owners is to control our dogs in neutral, or *calm* as I call it.

### Forward Gear

Forward gear comes with two options: excitement and aggression (a protective state of mind).

*Excitement* is when a dog moves toward someone or another dog, to greet them with excitement; he's wagging his tail, obviously happy and could even lick or jump on a person.

*Aggression* is when a dog moves toward someone or another dog, while in a dominant/aggressive state. He may be barking, growling, with his tail likely straight up like a flag; hackles (the hair along the top of a dog's back) could be raised; he may be very quiet with a fixated stare and stiff body, all with the intent of dominating, nipping or biting as a result.

When a dog is in a forward gear, an owner must *react* to their forward gear posturing and bring their pet's mindset back to neutral or *calm*. At any time, we can instigate or allow playful excitement while a dog is in a forward gear, but it is an owner's responsibility to manage their dog to avoid any negative behavior, e.g., jumping or bothering people or other dogs, and regain calm control. *Proactive management* keeps a dog in a calm mode before he reacts to someone or something and changes his energy from neutral to forward gear. This requires insight and awareness from an owner, who must be completely cognizant of all situations, from all directions.

Reverse Gear

Reverse gear is when a dog is nervous or insecure, often called a *Nervous Nellie*. It is the leader's job to give a nervous dog confidence that everything is OK. Dogs need to feel protected and safe, just like us.

In human terms, imagine that a young child is feeling scared and nervous on a dark stormy night, when there is a noise outside in the backyard, and a parent's reaction was to say to the child, "There are bad guys in the backyard; go outside and protect us." Another example; when walking down the street, you tell a child to protect you from other people and their dogs and encourage them to yell and scream at them to scare them away (similar to a barking, snarling dog). This would surely confuse the child, and if repeated, on a regular basis, would likely cause psychological problems. A parent's job is to make a child feel safe and protected – not the other way around.

Too often a *Nervous Nellie* is forced to take a forward position and protect the pack due to a void of leadership by their owner, even though they are not comfortable or competent at doing this. This is a double negative. It is one thing to be insecure and nervous (the first negative) but quite another to be expected to protect the pack as well (the second negative), often resulting in fear/aggression. When the leadership role isn't filled, he is obligated to take on the job of dominating and protecting the pack. The pack cannot be leaderless: if owners don't lead; then a dog must.

Neutral Gear

The Game of Canine is predicated on your being able to *control the calm to win the game*, under all circumstances. To be either proactive or reactive, the objective is to achieve a calm dog in neutral gear using calm, strong, leader-energy: within five seconds. This is how points are scored by dog owners.

# Chapter 5

## The Game of Canine

*Who's winning? What's the score?*

Imagine a game with a tall ladder – I call it the *Leader Ladder*. The Leader Ladder has 100 steps, which represent zero percent at the bottom to 100 percent at the top. When you've climbed to the top of the Leader Ladder, you are a winner at the Game of Canine. This means that you are a canine *purist,* implicitly and successfully implementing the eighteen rules of the Game of Canine, while enjoying living with a balanced dog. (All eighteen rules are in the next chapter).

Note: This is a game that everyone in the family can win, as each player individually competes against their opponent: their dog(s). Young children can share the Leader Ladder with adults and older siblings.

You will reach the top rung on the Leader Ladder *when* you are 100 percent leader of the pack. If you are 80 percent of the way up the ladder, then your dog is at 20 percent. Most dog owners would be elated with this result – nobody is perfect. Dogs are always at an inverse position to humans, on Leader Ladders. The only way to move your dog down to ten percent is for you to climb up to ninety percent, because *you cannot push your dog down the ladder, it is you who must climb higher.*

Whenever you score a point and climb up a step, your dog forfeits a point and drops down a step. Whenever he gains a point, it is at your expense, as you give up a point and drop down a step. Like the board game Snakes and Ladders, you can continuously rise and fall by going up and down your Leader Ladder with the objective of getting to the top, but never get there. You can also get to the top and hit the big long snake that takes you back to the bottom. Just as you can go from the top of your Leader Ladder to the bottom by changing from acting black or white (canine wave length) to gray (human wave length) and give up your high position on you ladder. Obviously, there are no dice; the only way to move up your Leader Ladder is to dominate and score points.

For example, when you calm your dog within five seconds, it is you who scores a point, while he gives up a point. If a dog controls his excitement for over five seconds, he scores a point, which means you lose a point. Every five seconds thereafter he scores another point. Therefore, in one minute of uncontrollable misbehavior, the score would be 12:0 for your dog – a shutout. To make matters worse, you'd have to give up 12 points resulting in a 24-point spread. This would be a major repositioning in the pecking order.

Any time you or another family/pack member is dealing with your dog, say he is barking at the front door; someone can call out to that person and ask, "Who is scoring points? Who is winning the game?" This will immediately bring their focus to the fundamentals of the game. When you view your dog as your opponent, just like any other game, it is easy to focus on the imaginary scoreboard and ask, "What's the score?"

*Calms* come in different degrees of intensity, and some easier to achieve than others. Whenever it takes a huge effort to calm your dog, the more compelling the point you earn while climbing your Leader Ladder, which equates to a bigger *mental* drop down the Leader Ladder for your dog. The *higher* your position on the Leader Ladder, the *lower* your dog's position will be. So, the greater the distance between the two of you on your Leader Ladder, the better you are playing the game (90:10 is significantly better than 60:40). This establishes your dominant position and earns your dog's respect. The tighter you follow the rules of the Game of Canine, the faster and higher, you climb your Leader Ladder.

In the wild canine world, the leader/alpha tenaciously remains at 100 percent on his/her Leader Ladder, while all other pack mates remain at zero. This never changes: it's always black or white; leader or follower. This natural and pure form of pack hierarchy is the law of canine nature, which we humans must aim to achieve within our combo-pack of dogs and humans.

It's totally natural for canines to instantly give their leader a calm, whenever given the order to do so. If the leader of a wild canine pack senses danger, he/she gives the danger signal and the whole pack freezes, stops whatever they are doing and goes quiet in lightning speed; the snap of a finger. A canine is also capable of going from a calm, quiet mood to 100 percent excited or aggressive in the same split-second time frame that it takes them to go back to calm. In the Game of Canine, five seconds is an eternity to your dog.

It's important to keep score. I remember my second visit to a family who had rescued a rather skittish, fearful and aggressive German Shepherd Dog. When I arrived at their door, the father was desperately trying to calm her down. Her misbehavior was minimal, compared with the first time I'd entered their home, but it was still a concern. I asked their son, who was standing next to me, "How long would you say that I've been here?" He said, "About 20 seconds." I loudly responded, "The score is 4:0 for your dog."

This caused an immediate reaction from the dad, who stepped close to the dog's nose and clapped his hands. The dog immediately became calm. I added, "Well done. The score is now 4:1. Why didn't you do that in the first place?" They all laughed and realized the importance of the imaginary scoreboard. The father looked over his shoulder and said to me, "Bruce, you couldn't have made this any simpler, could you?"

**Green-ring energy**

It is impossible to have a calm dog if you don't have calm-energy yourself. When we think of successful business leaders or political leaders, they are very calm, strong and confident. This is the same energy we must exude when leading our canine pack members.

How can such energy be measured? I don't know of any meter that measures human energy, so I use an abstract, humorous method. Imagine you're wearing a mood-ring. I use green to represent calm, strong leader-energy. Therefore, all other colors represent other energies, such as anger, fear, frustration, embarrassment, nervousness, anger, etc. A green ring shows that you have the calm, strong, energy of a leader. Either your ring is green, or it is not. (I'll refer to the green-ring concept throughout the book).

Dogs don't earn respect for each other, as humans do. Dogs *take* it aggressively. A fundamental with dogs is that they will give you anything you *demand*, but they will take everything they can get away with. There is a very fine line between the two. You cannot ask your dog, "Would you please go calm, sit or come?" Remember, just like in the military: "This is an order, Private Canine. No discussion or negotiations."

A direct order or command must be enforced by the human *general/alpha*. However, just like a teenager, your beloved canine will try to get away with absolutely everything he thinks he can. When giving your four-legged family member orders think green, as in green mood-ring. Leaders are always calm and strong, which is mandatory to have a calm dog.

# Chapter 6

## 18 Rules to the Game of Canine; a.k.a. *The Recipe*

*These become your new habits.*

Throughout the book I often refer to the rules of the Game of Canine as *The Recipe.*

It's like a recipe to bake a cake. If you follow the recipe accurately, you'll end up with a great cake every time. The same is true if you follow these eighteen Rules to the Game of Canine; you'll create and maintain balanced dogs for life. Of course, you must continually and consistently keep following the rules or your balanced relationship will revert to confusion, resulting in canine misbehavior: just as a cake recipe must be consistently and accurately followed.

The eighteen Rules to the Game of Canine are detailed in four specific chapters of this book. (See each chapter for complete explanation).

***Chapter 17; The Golden Rule:***

Tell them once and *never* take *no* for an answer. (This is the most important rule and merits a chapter of its own.)

***Chapter 19; Five Ways to Communicate in Canine:*** This list is in a descending order, with No. 5 being the least effective way to communicate with your dog.

1. Energy: the question is not *if* you are sending a message via your energy, it's *what* is your message?

2. Body language: Dogs express their thoughts and feelings using many different body parts, along with physical positions. We can also express ourselves utilizing some of their methods.

3. A leash: Your leash can be tight or loose; a loose leash is the objective.

4. Hand signals: Because dogs are stellar at reading each other physically, utilize this skill set and communicate with hand signals.

5. Words: Obviously dogs don't talk. They learn certain repeated sounds that we use, for example: come, sit, stay, etc. To increase your effectiveness when communicating with your dog, try focusing on No. 1 through 4, above.

***Chapter 24; Six Ways to Interrupt Negative Behavior:*** This list is in an ascending order of intensity, with No. 6 being the most assertive. Remember, "Less is always best." Try to use the least amount of assertion possible when interrupting your dog. The objective is to redirect their focus to you. Consider numbers one through four as a mini-explosion, very short in length.

1. Say, "Hey." A whisper is better than a yell.

2. Clap. This is a simple yet very effective form of interrupting.

3. Pop the leash. A light flick is usually all that is needed.

4. Simulate a bite. Try a light tap or poke in either bite zones, neck or belly.

5. Put your hand on their throat to simulate a *kill bite.* Under most conditions just touching them will suffice.

6. Either lift their front feet off the ground by grabbing their scruff (bitches carry their pups this way without hurting them) or push their chin to the ground/floor. I consider this to be the maximum assertion and should be used for only two reasons – aggression or insubordination.

***Chapter 29; Six Ways to Say, "I'm The Leader, Not You.":*** These rules are not listed in any hierarchical order. Through these six actions, you can show leadership ... or not.

1. "I lead the hunt (or walk)." In the wild, the alpha almost always leads the pack.

2. "I go in and out of doors first." The leader steps outside/inside the den to check for danger before calling the pack out/in.

3. "I eat first." The leader always eats before the rest of the pack. He must keep strong to lead and protect the pack.

4. "I control the door." When visitors arrive, you must be able to calm your dog, either near the door or anywhere else in the home. Of course, the objective is to get a *calm* within five seconds.

5. "I ignore my dog when arriving home." He/she must give you sixty seconds of respect before you acknowledge them.

6. "I live higher than my dog." No bed, no couch for man's best friend.

As mentioned, each of these eighteen rules is explained in detail within the four listed chapters in the book.

# Chapter 7

## Control the Calm to Win the Game

*Chaos is ineffective.*

**Three Ways to Score a Calm:**

**1. When going through an outside door.**

When your dog calmly passes through an outside door, either in or out, you score a point in the Game of Canine because you controlled the calm. The reason is that the leader in the canine world always goes through the door first to make sure there is no danger when going in or coming out of the den. Typical dog behavior when going outside is very excited, involving pulling and running ahead as they pass through the door before humans. Coming into the home usually isn't much different. By having a calm dog wait for you as you step out/in of the door first, to hypothetically ascertain a safe environment, until you give them the command to follow, you score a point. (This is also explained in number 2 of Chapter 29; "Six Ways to Say, I'm the Leader, Not You.")

**2. Changing behavior.**

Whenever you can alter the behavior of a dog, whether in forward or reverse gear, to become calm, in neutral gear, you score a point. In forward gear, the only difference between happy excitement and dominant/aggressive excitement is the result; a lick or a bite, be it toward another dog or human. For a detailed explanation (see Chapter 25; "Six Ways to Interrupt Negative Behavior.") Once calm is established within five seconds, you score a point and get to climb up your Leader Ladder one step, as your dog slips down one step. The same is said for controlling a nervous dog in reverse gear, e.g., when preventing him from nervously barking or running away. You must exude green-ring leader-energy to instill in him enough confidence that he senses your strength, knowing that you will protect him.

**3. Calmly control themselves.**

This is when your dog gives you a calm, by doing something calmly that they previously would have done with excitement or fear. For example, if the old habit for your dog was to bark and jump on visitors when entering your home and their new habit is to control themselves with no barking or jumping, you then get to count a calm and earn a point because of their new, composed behavior. Your dog may be sitting while his butt is in a constant state of motion, but he is controlling and containing himself.

These are the best points possible because your dog is doing all of the work by calmly controlling himself from going into forward or reverse gear. This is exactly what you are aiming to achieve, without much ado. You will swell with pride when your dog shows such high level of respect to you.

**When You Are in or Out of the Game**

Imagine athletes playing a sport. As soon as they step across the white line on the field or playing surface, they are *in or out of the game*. It's the same in the Game of Canine. Whenever you enter your home and see your dog, you are instantly *in the game,* just as when you leave your home without your dog, you are *out of the game.* The game never stops or ends while you are together – *never.*

Owners often ask me about going away on holidays and leaving their dog with someone else. "What will happen when we return?" My answer; "As soon as you enter the house, you will be back in the game. While you are away, the game will be between the dog and the dog sitter. Like children going to their grandparents' house while their parents are away on vacation, your child will be spoiled. In fact, it is their job to spoil their grandchildren.

Upon your return, when it's time for bed and your kids tell you that they stayed up much later at grandma and grandpa's house, you're likely to respond with, "You are now at home, not at grandma's and grandpa's, and must go by our rules." So, when you return home from your holiday and your dog is acting spoiled rotten, he's likely to have taken a dominant posture over the dog sitter or grandma. You then must immediately re-enforce the Eighteen Rules to the Game of Canine. Because these are your dog's rules, he will react very quickly to the changing of the guard.

## Chapter 8

## The Combo-Pack: Humans and Dogs

*One big happy family.*

As humans, we all know how to relate to one another because we all live by the laws of human nature. Dogs are the same – they innately know the laws of canine nature. It is only when the two species cohabit that confusion, on both parts, takes place. By learning to understand the canine way and act accordingly, behavioral problems dissipate, and harmonious balance is possible.

I am unbelievably fortunate to have an ideally balanced dog in my home. I often use Satchmo as an example of pack balance. This is not for self-glory, but simply to give reference to the behavior of a balanced dog. My goal is to pave the way for all dog owners to share the same joy living with balanced dogs. Creating a balanced pack is within all dog owners' grasp. By diligently following The Recipe, the result is predictable; a happy, balanced combo-pack of humans and dogs.

Balance in a canine world is when your dog shows you, their leader, total respect. He expects and counts on you to manage and protect the pack. He keeps track of you and lies in wait for your every command, as his job is to serve you. This is a life of mutually working together. Sometimes respect must be earned, while other times it must be taken. If a follower wolf didn't do as the leader instructed, there would be a physical confrontation, with the subordinate being put in his/her place. This would be when respect is taken. A dog will give you everything you demand – but take everything they can get away with.

Age is irrelevant: When an eight-week-old puppy, a two-year-old adult dog or a senior dog is rescued and comes into the family home, we welcome them all into the *Gray Zone*. Dogs do not view their leader as the one who pays the mortgage, puts food on the table or pays the vet bill. This obviously means absolutely nothing to the dog, and of course *everything* in this book is about a dog's point of view. As a new family member, he must immediately define the pack ranking. Who are the leaders? What other members are in the combo-pack? What position in the pack does each member hold?

He also needs to establish his own position in the pecking order. Most owners have no idea of the significance of hierarchy positioning to a dog. But if a dog does not recognize strong, consistent leadership, he will consider the pack to be in a state of flux, resulting in anarchy, where pack members are obligated to vie for the top position. Far too often a submissive dog is thrown into the leadership position; whether he's capable or not, because he perceives that no one else is filling the role and someone must do the job. This often causes fear/aggression with insecure dogs. The human leader(s) of the pack includes all family members, age not being a factor. Ideally a domestic dog should view all human pack members to be higher on the Leader Ladder than himself and therefore he will be subservient, respective and obey them all.

Obviously, a young child is not going to be able to dominate by himself. But an adult or older sibling can share the responsibilities with the young child. If a young child is not accompanied by a higher-ranking human pack member when giving a dog a command, the dog is likely to show disrespect and give the child a look that says, "You're not the boss of me." This is what young siblings often say to each other, accompanied by the same look.

**Human leaders have the same two specific jobs as a canine leader: to *dominate* and *protect* the pack.**

**1. Dominance** in the home consists of keeping pack balance in the hierarchy; controlling fighting, nipping, biting, guarding, excessive barking, jumping, soiling, pulling on the leash and anything else the leader perceives to be negative. The human alpha makes all pack decisions, e.g., when and where to go; when and what to eat; when to start playing and when to end the play; when to be quiet; when to give obedience commands, etc. It is the leader's job to control *all* aspects of the game.

**2. Protection** means the leader prevents both people and other dogs from hurting any pack member. If you're out walking with your dog and an unleashed stray dog approaches, it is your job, as leader, to shoo away the stray by stepping in front and keeping yourself between the two animals. If the stray comes near, yell at him, clap your hands, make some noise and let him know that you mean business, until he takes off and leaves you alone. Your dog will get a loud and clear message that you are his protector. Conversely, the human leader must also protect human pack members from their dog, especially children, just as they must protect their dog from children.

Posturing or ranking is a constant non-stop process of your dog evaluating your position on your Leader Ladder. Owners must assume the leader position like a four-star general. When the leader position is filled, only the follower rank remains. Therefore, by the process of elimination, a dog's only option is to be a follower.

**Has your dog been forced into the role of leader?**

**The following are examples of dominant behavior.**

**Your dog:**

- While on walks is out in front of you, pulling on the leash, sniffing or peeing (marking) frequently.
- Gets overly excited and cannot be settled when the doorbell rings.
- Barks or whines incessantly or becomes destructive when left alone (separation anxiety).
- Barks, mouths, growls, snarls, nips or bites family members or others.
- Soils in the home to mark his territory; this includes floors, beds, shoes or clothing of various family members.
- Guards food, bones, toys, a certain space or something he possesses.
- Follows someone around the home, so that he can keep track of them.
- Demands attention and jumps on either you or visitors when entering the home.

- Doesn't listen to you or won't come when called.
- Stands between you and other people, including other family members.

**The following are examples of protective behavior.**

**Your dog:**

- Barks at people, dogs, squirrels, cats, kids on bikes, skateboards, etc., while out on a walk, in the home or car.
- Aggressively barks, snarls, nips, bites or lunges at people or dogs.
- Continuously, and possibly aggressively, barks and growls and cannot be settled when the doorbell rings (same as dominant behavior).
- Barks while running around the perimeter of the yard, as if on border patrol.
- Stands between you and other people, including other family members. (same as dominant behavior)

A balanced dog will not show any of the above behaviors. How does the song go? **R-E-S-P-E-C-T.** It is only when a dog owner understands canine psychology that a balanced pack and a happy household can be achieved and enjoyed. Follow The Recipe to achieve the following: realign the pack hierarchy to create a balanced pack; clearly fill the role of a leader; communicate effectively in the language of canine; tell your dog that you are the leader versus telling him that he's the leader; proactively manage and lead the pack; interrupt negative behavior using canine techniques.

## Chapter 9

## Canine Hierarchy – Ranking –Pecking Order

*It's easy to earn your stars and stripes.*

The most important thought on a dog's mind is ranking, a.k.a. posturing, the pecking order, or hierarchy. These words are all synonyms in the Game of Canine. To stop a dog from ranking would be like trying to stop gravity – it's impossible. Ranking is perpetual and cannot be turned off, however, it will soften in their senior years.

Dogs are hardwired for this purpose. Why do male dogs lift their leg to pee? Answer: To appear bigger than they are, by leaving their mark higher on a tree or pole. In a wild canine pack, the only male to lift his leg is the alpha. All other males must squat to pee. The reason is that when other wolves/animals come into a pack's territory, it is the alpha's scent that is smelled; he is considered the ruler of his territory and it is he who will protect it. This is stringently enforced by the alpha.

When dogs smell the scent of another dog's pee on the ground, they commonly pee on top of it to leave their mark. Both genders do this. They can't not do it. It is common for a dog to scratch the ground after they defecate, or sometimes when they pee, because they have scent glands in the pads on their feet that also express their personal scent. Why do dogs have anal glands? These glands express a liquid scent on their stool. Each time a dog defecates they leave their distinct mark.

All the above is solely for marking their territory or *leaving their calling card.*

When dogs meet each other, they have an explicit system of ranking or posturing. The most significant way is via energy; they are like superheroes at communicating this way. They can read each other's energy without even seeing each other from an amazing distance; it's a natural survival technique. Physically, there are several obvious levels of posturing amongst themselves. Staring is a physical starting point, as dogs send and receive messages. They will also put their chin or head over the other dog's shoulders or withers, just behind the neck. The next physical level occurs when a dog puts his front leg over another dog's back, almost like a loose head lock but over their back. If the dominant dog is smaller than the other dog, he will stand on his hind legs and put his front paws on the larger, less dominant dog's ribcage or hind leg if he can't reach their body.

I witnessed Satchmo do this with a large Rottweiler when he was about 10 weeks old. He stood on his hind legs with his front paws on the Rottie's rib cage to show dominance. They proceeded to play and run around the yard. When the Rottie lay down on his side, or prone position, for a rest, Satchmo climbed up on him and sat on his ribcage, with all feet off the ground, showing his *top-dog* status. It is not uncommon for a smaller dog, say a Yorkshire Terrier, to dominate a Great Dane or another much larger dog through their energy, as they do not think about size, unlike humans.

The next level of domination would be for a dog to hump the subordinate dog. This is not sexual but an act of dominant posturing.

This level of posturing can often cause the subordinate dog to retaliate with aggression. Dogs often hump people as well. This distinct expression of dominance, often laughed at, is a serious matter to a dog.

# **Chapter 10**

## **Satchmo**

*A.k.a. Louis Armstrong.*

When I began my hobby of studying dog psychology, which eventually became my career, I didn't own a dog. I lived in a no-pet building. Ultimately, I decided that I needed a dog/partner to be more effective in my work. So, I moved. Then, I had to decide on a breed that best suited my needs. Choosing the wrong breed can create endless problems for a dog owner, just as making the correct choice can immeasurably enhance your life for many years.

When picking your dog, I believe the first criteria to consider is the compatibility of energy levels. Look for a dog that has a similar energy level to you. Don't pair up with a high-energy dog if you don't have an active lifestyle and vice versa. If you already have a dog and want to add another dog to your pack, pick one with an energy level similar to or lower than your present dog.

My needs were a little different than most. I needed a working dog, one that was typically bred for military or police work. This type of dog is known for its confidence, intelligence, being good with people and ability to be both harsh and soft in any situation. By harsh or soft I mean that they can deal with the harsh, demanding needs of either police or military work one minute, and then in the next minute they can be soft and snuggly with a young child. In my case the energy level was not the primary consideration, although most working breeds tend to be high-energy dogs. My mandate was finding a dog with tremendous confidence to help the unbalanced dogs that I work with.

My next criterion was to select a non-shedding breed, since I'd decided that I wanted to live without dog hair in my home. This left me with a very short list. There are a number of non-shedding breeds, but very few of them fall into the class of a working dog. For example; Poodles, Doodles, Portuguese Water Dogs, Barbets, Soft Coated Wheaten Terriers and a plethora of other breeds all make wonderful pets, and I recommend all of them to anyone in the need of a non-shedding dog. My problem is that they are not classified as working dogs (other than the Portuguese Water Dog, which was created to work in the water around ships, but not for military and police work).

The list of non-shedding working dogs is extremely limited. The shortlist for me was; Black Russian Terrier, Bouvier des Flandres, Standard Schnauzer and Giant Schnauzer. All four excel in the working-dog category. The Giant Schnauzer seemed best suited to my needs because they are stellar on both sides of the harsh/soft requirement list. Their exceptional ability to be soft with anyone, especially children, was most attractive to me. Another deciding factor was their love for water. It is always fun to hang out at a lake with a dog who loves to swim and play in water. The Giant Schnauzer breed has been considered a purebred since the early 1800s. They are a combination of Great Danes, Bouvier des Flandres, Shepherds and Standard Schnauzers.

It took me several months of studying to investigate and learn about specific breeds before I'd chosen mine. Next, I had to find a breeder of choice. The Giant Schnauzer being an uncommon breed, this task was far more onerous than one would expect. There are two distinct bloodlines to choose from: North American and European.

The harsher European bloodline is often used for Schutzhund competition. Schutzhund was originally created as a test to evaluate police and military dogs, and today it is a competitive worldwide sport. It includes obedience, tracking and guard work that requires a very high prey-drive in a dog.

The North American bloodline is popular in confirmation competition; this is a contest among dogs of each breed as to how well they represent their breed standards prepared by each breed association; it could also be referred to as a beauty contest of the breed. These dogs tend to make better pets, as they are less harsh. My choice was the North American bloodline.

I already had the name picked out; it was my nickname as a teenager. I was a trumpet player and my father used to call me Satchmo. I can still hear him calling me for dinner when I was practicing my horn after school, "Hey, Satchmo, dinner's ready." Satchmo was the nick-name of Louis Armstrong, a great jazz trumpeter, hence the moniker. Satchmo's nickname is Louis Armstrong. He answers to either.

Like all dogs, while Satchmo lived with his siblings and mother she was the 100 percent leader of her pack. Her job was to make all the decisions and protect them with her life. When he came into my home, where I am 100 percent leader of my pack, it was natural for him to remain at zero on the Leader Ladder. This is the ideal relationship between owner and dog, which all owners should aim to achieve.

Because of his confident gene pool, Satchmo keeps a constant pressure on me, which I must continually mitigate. If I slack off by only a smidgen, he pushes the dominant envelope and I then must react to maintain a healthy balance within my pack.

This control of pack balance or hierarchy began immediately upon his arrival in my home and it never stops, as pack posturing is a basic law of canine nature.

I didn't expect Satchmo to work with me until he was at least 10 months old. But I was wrong in that expectation. He started working with me at three months and has been stellar at his job ever since. By communicating calm, strong energy to each of my clients' dogs, with no fear or aggression, he helps them to achieve the same balanced energy.

Throughout the book I talk about green-ring energy. As I've mentioned, a green colored mood-ring represents calm, strong leader-energy, while other ring colors represent different moods; e.g., anger, fear, frustration, nervousness, ticked off, etc. Satchmo is the epitome of green-ring energy. If he had fingers, I'd buy him a green mood-ring.

If a dog tries to bite or lunge toward him, he jumps back to avoid a bite and then immediately returns to his original place and calmly waits. He doesn't show aggression or fear toward the other dog. If the dog repeats his aggression, he again jumps back like a rabbit and then he often turns around and approaches backward or comes in sideways and raises his hind leg, as if to say, "I have no fear or aggression. Go ahead, you have the first smell."

I can't imagine if someone tried to hurt me that I would turn my back to them and then approach them again walking backwards. Sometimes he will approach an aggressive dog and immediately swing his butt into the dog's face or turn sideways and lift his hind leg. Both approaches let the other dog smell him first. Typically, the dog that smells first takes the dominant stance. Satchmo naturally lets the other dog have the dominant position. Not all dogs want to be top-dog, which is evident very quickly. Satchmo never fights for this position and is quite content for another dog to be strong and confident as well. No dog is higher in posturing than him, but he is OK with any dog being as high-as-he-is. He does this more so while working.

When not working and he meets dogs on the street or while at a local park, he postures with them differently. If the other dog senses his non-threatening energy they seem to get along very quickly. Whenever a dog expresses fear or aggression, Satchmo usually ignores them and walks away.

The potent combination of his DNA and his balance provides him with the level of confidence and overall chutzpah that are well beyond anything that I could have imagined. I never dreamed that he would be anywhere near as effective as he is when working. He instinctively knows when it is time to work. I wish that I could take credit for his astonishing behavior. I can only take credit for implementing the ideal balance within my pack. Satchmo is innately cognizant of the fact that my job is to protect him, which naturally enhances his confidence.

I normally introduce Satchmo on my second session with clients to help them learn how to maintain a calm dog. Satchmo becomes the decoy or distraction for their dog, which creates an opportunity for my clients to score points in the Game of Canine. The way that I typically introduce Satchmo is to have him calmly wait in the back of my station wagon. I ask the clients to stand a short distance back from the vehicle and I then pop open the tailgate. Satchmo is trained to stay in the car and not jump out. He must also remain totally calm and quiet, no whining or barking.

The mission of the client is to achieve and maintain their dog in a calm mode and keep moving forward toward Satchmo. The ideal is for them to progress as close as possible to the rear bumper. The intensity increases exponentially as they progress closer to Satchmo. Achieving and maintaining a *calm* can be considered a huge victory for most dog owners, as dogs may be excited and want to play, aggressive and want to fight, or nervous and want to get the heck out of there. Most dogs are happy to sniff Satchmo nose to nose and many jump into the car with him, as he welcomes all.

The following three chapters are examples of Satchmo at work; they highlight the benefits of pack balance and how significant the ranking process is to dogs. Pack balance eliminates hierarchy confusion, which is the common cause of canine misbehavior, the self-inflicted curse of far too many dog owners.

## Chapter 11

## Satchmo's First Day on the Job

*This age would be considered child labour to us.*

When Satchmo was three months old, I was working with a family and their Airedale named Barney. The owners, Gordon and Cathy, had spent several thousand dollars on vet bills of many neighbours' dogs, who had been on the receiving end of 'Cujo' Barney's aggressive attacks. Gordon and Cathy were not in good standing in their neighbourhood. There was obvious tension whenever they were outside with Barney. The scorn and disrespectful looks from their neighbours added to their embarrassment when walking their uncontrollable attack-dog.

The good news is that once Barney was in balance and his family practiced the rules to the Game of Canine, it was only a matter of time before the healing process between neighbours took place.

On my second visit I was positively impressed by how far Cathy and Gordon had progressed with the now non-Cujo Barney. He was totally respectful when I rang the doorbell; only a couple of barks to let them know that I was there, and then he went calm as Cathy took control and answered the door. We had a wonderful conversation about how they were now winning the Game of Canine, along with details of how well their walks were going. Things weren't perfect yet, but the level of improvement was very impressive. Cathy and Gordon had a serious reason to get a handle on their situation, and they both stepped up to achieve terrific results.

Barney's level of dog aggression had dropped to about 10 percent of his norm. He only showed minimal signs of any barking or pulling as dogs approached, including his two aggressive arch rivals from across the street. This level was easily controlled. Cathy or Gordon stopped and stood in front of him whenever a dog approached and were able to calm him in short order and score all the points. This was life-changing to them as their embarrassment turned to pride. They were blown away by the level of control they gained in such a short period of time. Suddenly Barney had a new name, 'Gentleman' Barney.

We went outside so that I could watch Gentleman Barney at his new best. He was awesome while Cathy walked him. With timing that I could not have planned any better, their neighbour from across the street appeared with her two small and very yappy Chihuahuas, Barney's two nemeses. Both dogs were hyper and wailing at fever pitch. Cathy easily scored a point as she managed to control *the calm.* I quickly call out to the neighbour, "Excuse me, would you please stop and wait for a minute as we are training Barney?" She was accommodating and stopped with her two non-stop barking little rascals.

I asked Cathy if she would like to see Barney at his very best. She was all for whatever I had in mind. I took the leash, crossed the street with Barney and stopped in the middle of the road. *Frick and Frack* were beside themselves with uncontrollable barking and aggression. I next proceeded to the edge of the curb, which was quite close to them as they stood on the boulevard. Gentleman Barney stayed calm, cool and collected as he remained in his balanced, quiet and respective mode. I thanked the neighbour for her help in the demonstration and we returned to Cathy. The woman called out to me, "What kind of drugs is Barney on? I should get some for my crazy pair." I turned toward her and of course told her that he was drug-free.

Barney's turnaround behavior was so impressive that I suggested we bring Satchmo out of the car and introduce the two of them. Cathy immediately said, "I don't think that is a good idea. I don't want any more vet bills if Barney hurts him." I said, "I'll take responsibility." As I approached them with Satchmo, I noticed Barney fixating on him. I then suggested to Cathy that we switch dogs.

As Barney and I approached Cathy and Satchmo, Barney let out a quick bark followed by a deep warning growl. Satchmo stood his ground and didn't show any signs of stress or fear. I corrected Barney's showing of aggression with a quiet 'Hey' sound along with a light pop of his leash, which interrupted his focus and redirected it to me. He instantly went calm, so I moved closer to Satchmo a second time.

This time Barney dropped to the play-bow, with elbows on the ground, his butt in the air, and gave a quick jump. All of this said to me, "Let's play Satchmo." I then instructed Cathy to drop Satchmo's leash as I dropped Barney's. Both dogs proceeded to run around the front yard and wrestle playfully.

I watched as tears ran down Cathy's cheeks. "I can't believe that your little dog could bring Barney out of his aggressive mode and get him to play, she said. "He hasn't played with another dog for years. He must be in heaven."

We let Satchmo and Barney play until they were both worn out, with their tongues hanging out the side of their mouth.

I went back the next week, even though his owners didn't need me to, just to let Gentleman Barney play with Satchmo again. I put Satchmo in their yard and asked Cathy to let Barney out the back door. The fact that it was his yard and Satchmo was on his property was a big test for Barney. I stayed in close proximity, with a watchful eye. No problems arose, and the two dogs had a fun time wearing each other out once again.

From that day forward Satchmo has been a working dog first, and a pet second. Fortunately for me he is stellar in both categories. Coupled with his confidence and balance, he makes my job much more effective. He has taught me first-hand an enormous amount about dog behavior that I could never learn from a book. I never imagined how impactful he would be with dogs.

# Chapter 12

## Satchmo and an Aggressive Puppy

*Age is not a factor in posturing.*

I once worked with a young five-month-old Chocolate Lab by the name of Jasper, who was extremely confused about the pecking order in his pack. This resulted in an amazing amount of aggression toward just about anyone or anything, people and animals. It was heart wrenching to see such a young dog so far out of balance and living with so much stress. His owners were equally stressed. They told me, sadly, that I was his last chance; unless I could change his behavior, they would have to get rid of him.

I have heard that expression far too many times. It only makes me more determined to be successful for all those involved, both canines and humans. The good news is that all dogs accept being balanced, as did Jasper, because it is natural for them. Jasper accepted me as the new top dog soon after I arrived, but not without a short battle of wills. This meant that he was fired from the job as the dominant protector of his pack and relegated to that of a follower. He was elated with his job change.

His owners were two couples who were sharing a home; Mitchell and Roseanne along with Harry and Nava. Collectively they had enough arm and hand wounds to keep a bandage company in business.

It's amazing to see a dog psychologically do a 180-degree turn around in mindset within only a few short minutes and maintain this new position for life. This is predicated on his human owners consistently filling his needs of strong leadership.

Part of Jasper's misbehavior was due to a lack of socialization. He had been taken from his mother and litter mates when only five weeks old. The prime age to socialize a puppy is between eight to twelve weeks, because this is their most impressionable age. But it doesn't mean that socialization in impossible after this period. It may be a little more difficult, but the process requires the same approach – patience.

To socialize dogs means to introduce them to as many things as possible. This includes people of different sizes, ages, genders, races, clothing, even those dependent upon wheelchairs, walkers, canes, as well as other dogs, the vet or animal hospital, loud trucks, strange noises, skateboards, bicycles, motorcycles, lawn mowers, strange smells and anything else that you can think of. On garbage day, I followed close behind the garbage and recycling trucks for a few blocks with Satchmo. I also stopped at construction sites and simply stood by and did nothing but watch as big, noisy trucks rumbled past.

Another idea is to introduce elevators or escalators. They can be scary for a pup. I took Satchmo into the mall on many occasions to ride the escalator. They're weird for people, never mind four-legged dogs. No one ever gave me a hard time or asked me to leave. Think outside the box when socializing your pup. Unfortunately, Jasper had very little, if any, socialization.

By my second visit Jasper was predominantly more subservient to his human owners, more so with three of them. Jasper was still a puppy full of energy, but almost all his nipping and biting had subsided, and he was much more controlled. Mitchell was the weak link in the group, because he liked to be a playmate to Jasper and gave into him far too easily. There was very little *firm love* from Mitchell. Jasper needed this firm love to maintain his balance. Once this fact was discussed, Mitchell realized that he needed to tighten up on the rules of the Game of Canine. He was certainly higher on his Leader Ladder than before I'd first arrived, but it was imperative that he climb even higher, not only for his sake, but for Roseanne, Harry, and Nava as well.

We all went outside so they could show me how well walking with Jasper had progressed. Jasper was amazing with all but Mitchell, who he disrespectfully tried to pull all over the place. Dogs' black or white factor means that they either show respect or disrespect. There's no in between. Hopefully our previous talk in the house was enough for Mitchell to realize that he needed to step up and improve his game. Three-quarters of pack balance is not enough so I told them that I'd be back to follow up on Mitchell's progress. Total balance with all pack members was necessary to unequivocally maintain Jasper's new follower position.

At this point I decided it would be ideal to test Jasper with Satchmo. He was doing great with most of four humans. How about other dogs? Nava had him leashed and was about a car length back from my car. I popped the tailgate and within a couple of seconds Satchmo let out a low, rumbling growl. It was not a growl of aggression but a response to Jasper's posturing. At first, I was somewhat taken aback because Satchmo typically presents himself without any fanfare; just his friendly, calm self. I immediately looked at Jasper so that I could assess the whole picture and noticed his hackles up at the base of his tail. He also was leaning forward, with his weight on his front feet, while fixating on Satchmo. All these physical signs are an expression of dominant aggression. I then interrupted Satchmo with a 'Hey' sound and had him lie down while he remained in the car.

Next, I said to the four owners, "Your dog is giving off a message of dominant posturing and Satchmo is reacting to it." I then pointed out all of Jasper's physical signs of aggression. I also mentioned the most important message that we could not see, the aggressive energy that only Satchmo could detect. Satchmo's response was a low grumble, as if to say to Jasper, "Don't get cocky with me, young man."

I asked Nava to interrupt Jasper with a light sideways pop of the leash and to step in close to his snout. He was still fixated on Satchmo, so I suggested that she do a U-turn and then circle back again. This interrupted and redirected his thoughts and energy toward her, and he no longer showed signs of aggression to Satchmo.

By redirecting a dog's focal point back to us and away from what they are fixated on, positive results can be achieved with remarkably little effort.

Once all parties were calm, canines and humans, I brought Satchmo out of the car. At times like this I always start from a short distance and progressively move closer. Each time I stop, both dogs must remain calm. Once the dogs are close and showing signs of acceptance of each other, with no fixation, no raised hackles, a calm tail, and curiously sniffing the air toward each other, I let them meet.

At this critical point, as dogs are sizing up each other, problems arise if both dogs insist on being the top-dog or the highest on the Leader Ladder. Both can be dominant, confident and strong dogs who are OK with the other being the same, without fighting. However, some dogs can't handle Satchmo's strength and react with aggression. It is often the nervous, insecure young dog that gives off aggressive energy to try and make his case for being tough, much like a peacock that puffs up its feathers to appear bigger and more formidable, like Jasper.

I gave Satchmo the signal to approach Jasper. He immediately moved close to Jasper and stood with his head over his shoulders. This is the maximum level of dominance that Satchmo is allowed to express with dogs, whether he's working or not working. Nava said to me, "This is exactly what Jasper needs, to be put in his place." I agreed and reminded them all of my first visit when I established my dominance, which is exactly what Satchmo was doing as he stood over Jasper to make his point loud and clear. Jasper and Satchmo got along famously from that point on, "Game on, let's play."

It was another working day for Satchmo, as he helped Jasper find his place in the pack. Satchmo and I do the same thing with other dogs; we balance them. The difference is that he talks the talk, naturally, and much better than I do.

## Chapter 13

## Satchmo and Vickie: a Blind Dog

*They don't feel pity for each other.*

The call of panic came from Graham and Peggy, an English couple who had rescued a blind Bull Terrier. It led to one of the most emotional and gratifying dog-whispering experiences that I have experienced. Compounded with her blindness, Vickie was extremely head strong and immensely confused. She was a Hurricane Katrina rescue dog who, up to this point, had a very rough life.

Vickie had several serious issues, including biting, soiling and spinning. The biting part was the most serious misbehavior. Her owners had previously talked to their vet who suggested an antidepressant, but they rejected that. Graham and Peggy told me that they were at their wits' end and called me as their last hope. If I could not bring Vickie around, the plan was to euthanize her; they couldn't watch her suffer any longer.

I completely understood. One look at Peggy's arms amplified the biting story. A Bull Terrier has one of the most powerful jaws in the dog world. Their bite can consist of their locking onto your hand or arm and not letting go for several minutes. When this happens, it is impossible to get free without causing serious damage to your body. The best strategy; not the easiest, mind you, is to hold still until the dog lets go. Biting often occurred when Vickie refused to enter or exit her crate. If Graham or Peggy tried to put Vickie in her crate at night or get her out in the morning, it was battle mode for Vickie. Snarling, snapping, growling and biting were her standard Modus Operandi. Of course, she sensed the fear of her owners whenever this took place.

Another prime time for aggression was when she went into her *spinning* routine. This frequently took place when Graham or Peggy came home or if someone else came to visit. With visitors the doorbell was her trigger, and if they tried to stop her she would bite them. Their battle scars were prolific.

When I arrived, I was blown away at the insanity of Vickie's spinning, like a dog chasing its tail but much faster. The frenzy made my heart ache. I couldn't imagine how much stress she must be living with to exhibit such irrational behavior. I never know what I am going to encounter when I enter people's homes, but this time I was taken aback. I don't have a set plan when I meet dogs, I only react to what I am presented with. I knew that I had to interrupt her and make her stop.

There was no chance of her relaxing while a flurry of white fur kept going around and around. As she hit her head on a chair and then a cupboard, it was apparent that she was destined to hurt herself. I remember thinking that it was a good thing she was a Bull Terrier because they have a very distinct, massive forehead with not much flesh under her skin. By design, they are built to use their heads during battle.

I had very few options other than to grab her, hold her down and keep her still. Of course, one wants to hug and console a dog like Vickie to try and make her feel better, except that she is not a child. It took about 15 minutes for her to finally give in and relax.

It was a fight of great intensity that included a lot of growling and snarling with Vickie trying her best to bite me. I was lucky to come out with all my fingers. It was a hot, humid July day. I was sweating profusely. When she finally gave in and submitted to me I was happy and relieved. I think it was due to her getting tired, sensing that I was not trying to hurt her in any way, and that I was not backing off. My green-ring energy needed to be extra calm and strong for her, with no pity, no anger.

Once Vickie relaxed and went calm, I had a drink of water and headed to the kitchen table, where I could teach Graham and Peggy the Game of Canine. On the way I stopped at Vickie's water bowl, so she could have a much-needed drink. Vickie had been a determined and dominant champion of Game of Canine when playing against Graham and Peggy, who weren't much competition. Vickie was now lying down beside me; she immediately went on her side in the prone position, with her tongue hanging out the side of her mouth.

I explained to Graham and Peggy that there are four levels of calm for a dog; standing, sitting, lying down with her belly on the floor, and finally lying on her side in a prone position, which is the maximum level of calm. Vickie was naturally enjoying her new position as 100 percent follower, a first since she arrived in their home. Sometimes a fight is necessary to bring a positive end; with dogs and people.

As Peggy and Graham sat at the table, it was evident that they were deeply moved by the battle that just took place. To watch their family member go through this intense process to achieve a feeling of calm was bittersweet for them. They were like parents feeling for their child, and their pity was intensified because of Vickie's blindness. They were speechless. Both wiped away their tears as they witnessed, for the first time, a Vickie who was not tense, nervous and on-guard. They felt Vickie's contentment as she calmly lay beside me. I let the new energy in the room sink in and didn't push forward with my lessons for a few minutes because this historical moment was powerful and emotional.

Graham and Peggy both reveled at Vickie's new, relaxed demeanour. Both spoke quietly through their tears about the new energy in the room. Peggy said that she believed I'd been sent to them by a higher being. I said, "I was just the final cog in the process to save Vickie. You guys started it when you so unselfishly rescued a blind dog. You are special people to rescue a dog with significant issues."

"We had no idea what we were about to get into when we chose Vickie at the animal shelter," Graham said. "In fact, we believe that she chose us, not the other way around. The process has been a constant roller coaster between love and hate. We both love her so much, but we also are afraid of her and are continuously fluctuating emotionally. One minute we are hugging her, the next she is biting us and we, of course, get angry. We both have had at least ten bites that have drawn blood. All of that being said; I can't believe how calm I feel at this moment."

Vickie only once tried to move from her place on the floor beside me as I taught two very attentive, smiley and happy dog owners the Game of Canine. I gave her a soft whisper 'Hey' sound and she immediately returned to a down position. I can't imagine the sense of relief that Vickie must have been experiencing. My guess is that she had not been this content in the many years of living without sight.

One would assume that because Vickie was blind that I would need to use lots of words to communicate with her. That was not the case and reiterates that energy is the No. 1 way to communicate with canines. Even though she was blind I did not talk to her. I suggested that they use sounds, especially when walking her, to get their message across. I also suggested that they don't talk to her for several days. This would force them to focus on their energy which Vickie was acutely sensitive to. They needed for her to believe in their calm, green-ring energy. It was OK to say come, sit, stay and down.

They could add the words, "Curb up," as they dragged their left heel (she walked on their left side) to create a sound to communicate a curb was ahead (this would eliminate the banging of her front paws on the curb); a right heel drag along with saying, "Curb down," would indicate a step down off a curb. Very quickly a slight foot drag of either foot would suffice to indicate a curb either up or down. They could also use these two feet drag sounds as they approached the stairs on the back porch; going both up and down. Vickie's hearing was no doubt piqued, as would all components of her sensory system.

It was the chit chat and baby talk of Graham and Peggy that I wanted to eliminate so that they focused on their energy, use of the leash and critical one-word messages. I also suggested that if they could whistle it would add another form of audio communication. It turned out that neither of them could whistle.

Upon my second visit with the newly balanced family pack, I had the rewarding and special pleasure of watching and hearing about Vickie's new balanced life.

"Now, she goes in or out of her crate with ease," Peggy said. "She hasn't pooped in the house or started spinning since your visit. Also, no bites. She's totally relaxed while walking beside us and content to be led by either of us. She doesn't bark at people or try to run away at various noises. She sometimes even lies down beside us if we stop and chat with a neighbour. When the doorbell rings, she gives a couple of barks. She perks up, wagging her tail, while anticipating meeting people."

"Compared to her previous behavior, she's purely positive and enjoyable. She explores the whole yard, sniffs and plays with us."

"I love it when a plan comes together," I said. "It's music to my ears. Even though I expect these results, it is endearing to witness." We all headed outside as I wanted to introduce Vickie to Satchmo, who was patiently waiting in the car. Boy, this was one time I wished I had a videographer handy to catch the magic that was about to happen.

I had Graham stand about half a car length back from my car as I popped the tailgate open. (I usually have people with their dogs stand farther back when meeting Satchmo, but I wanted Vickie to smell as well as sense him with ease.) I anticipated that she would not react in a negative way by trying to get away or stand behind Graham. It was impressive to watch how she instinctively became aware of Satchmo. She immediately stared in his direction, even though she couldn't see.

While leaning on her front feet with her ears perked forward, she started sniffing the air, which is a very positive sign of curiosity. She just stood still with her tail down, to indicate her calm respect to Satchmo; her tail was not tucked under with fear. Satchmo was his usual self and stood calmly as he sniffed and stared at Vickie.

I suggested to Graham that if Vickie started to move in Satchmo's direction that he should allow her to do so. As if on cue, Vickie started to curiously move toward him. She stopped as she nudged the rear bumper of my car and lifted her head toward Satchmo, who was lying down and stretching his neck as far as he could without falling out of the car. Their noses touched, and both of their tails were wagging with excitement. I took some pictures of this special moment.

Next, I leashed Satchmo to bring him out of the car, so they could have a proper meeting. Vickie was a little apprehensive for the first few seconds as Satchmo stood above her posturing himself as if to say, "I'm strong, with no aggression or fear. You are safe; don't worry I won't hurt you; I'm here to help you with your recovery." He instinctively knew exactly how to handle the situation. Vickie very quickly brought her tail up as they both commenced with the dog sniffing routine. Satchmo let Vickie have the first smell. (This tends to relax and build confidence with nervous dogs.)

This was a brand-new experience for Vickie, as she had not met any dogs in the time that Graham and Peggy had owner her. Once again, my eyes welled up as I looked at Graham and Peggy. They also had tears in their eyes. My tears were a combination of my pride in Satchmo and happiness for Vickie and her family pack.

All sets of strong leadership energy; Satchmo's, mine, Graham and Peggy's, gave Vickie confidence and balance. The previous inconsistent and confusing energy of Graham and Peggy had now dissipated, creating a healthy balance in Vickie's mind. Satchmo brings the core element of the canine way. He naturally has enormously more impact than Bruce the human.

Next, I was able to witness Vickie walking up and down the street with Peggy with her new sense of being. She was not nervous or afraid, and it was truly a beautiful sight to watch this blind dog confidently letting Peggy lead her with a new level of trust and respect. Anyone watching would never notice Vickie's handicap. Peggy was beaming from ear to ear with pride and joy.

Boy, do I love my work. I am blessed to have such a special job. It can't get much more rewarding in the dog world than this.

As I followed up with Peggy a couple of weeks later, she reported that Vickie was progressing beautifully and that all was well within their pack. The crate issues, biting, soiling, spinning and doorbell aggression continued to be nonexistent. Vickie remained a balanced blind dog. Graham and Peggy are proud owners and deserve a medal for rescuing her. Their real reward is the love and enjoyment Vickie will bring them for many years to come. They now realize why they were drawn to rescue her. My reward was playing a part in Vickie's turnaround.

## Chapter 14

## Never Take Your Dog Out of the Game

*Keep me in the game, Coach.*

It is quite common for dogs to misbehave while greeting visitors at the door. They bark, jump, nip, bite, run out the door, etc., so their owners put them in another room, behind a gate or tether them to a banister or doorknob. This is taking your dog out of the game.

And it's too bad for a couple of reasons. Your dog cannot participate in the welcoming process when someone is at the door. One of the main reasons that people acquire a dog is for protection; your dog can't do much protecting if he's not with you at the door.

Even if your dog regularly misbehaves when answering the door (or anywhere else for that matter), keep her on a leash so that you can control her, but don't take her out of the game. The bottom line of this book is to control *the calm*, anytime, anyplace and in any situation. Often answering the door is a major problem area for dogs, who may bark uncontrollably and misbehave (See rule No. 4 in Chapter 29; "Six Ways to Say, I'm the Leader, Not You" for more details regarding answering the door).

If your dog is uncontrollable while you're answering your door, I suggest you work on some basic obedience training. The main three commands to focus on are; come, sit and stay. Try giving 25 commands per day. As your proficiency increases, so will your control at the door. The ideal is to leash your dog and have her in a sit/stay position; about eight feet back from the door, as visitors arrive.

What if the person at the door is a threat or a bad-guy with negative intentions? If your dog is not in the game, he'll be unable to back you up. Your dog will likely let you know that the person at the door is an unsavory character, well before you recognize it yourself. If you are ever concerned about a person at the door, put your dog between you and the threat while she is leashed. She will likely keep the visitor at bay by snarling and growling. Even a small dog will be a significant deterrent when she is in the protection mode.

I once met a lady who owned an Akita. One day an acquaintance was visiting her in her home. As the dog sat by the back door, the visitor said to her as she was making coffee, "Your dog seems to want to go outside. Do you want me to let him out for you?" She said, "Yes, please," and he let the dog out into the yard. He then proceeded to rape her, while the dog was locked outside and could not back her up or protect her. He was out of the game. "Keep me in the game, Coach."

# Chapter 15

## My Favorite Question; "When Did I Give Up Control?"

*Pay attention.*

You can ask yourself this question in any situation. It's an owner's responsibility to keep control of their dogs in all circumstances. Losing control of a dog can result from a simple turn of your head. When your dog is not in your view, she can act in a negative way without your realizing it. Imagine that you are answering the door and your dog sometimes runs outside when the door opens and other times she either jumps on visitors or nips their pant legs. If you give up your view of her as you focus on your visitors, she then has a few seconds head start on you to act in a negative fashion.

At that point you must react to her negative behavior and bring her back to calm; or you could have to chase her down the street. It's hands down easier and far more efficient to proactively manage your dog. Anticipating and keeping your eye on her will eliminate giving up control. Turning sideways while answering the door gives you a peripheral view of both the visitors and your dog with a simple turn of the head. You can talk to your guests while keeping an eye on your dog. This minimizes loss of control.

A mother with a small child walking down a busy street would not give up focus or control of the child because of the potential negative ramifications. Equally, as a dog owner, you must not lose focus or control of your dog. It is not only your job, it's also your responsibility.

The answer to the question, “When did I give up control?”, must emphatically be – “I didn’t.”

## Chapter 16

## Control Both Ends of the Situation

*Take charge. Be proactive.*

Our objective is to have total control over our dogs. Sometimes we also have to control other people and/or their dogs.

I was once working with a young couple, Steven and Emma, along with their aggressive Irish Setter, Paddy. I asked them not to make eye contact with him. This meant they could easily watch Paddy, but he could not visually connect with them and try to pull-them-in with his soft melting eyes. He was segregated and on his own with me as I took over the pack, from his point of view.

As the couple and I sat at the dining room table, Steven kept looking under the table at the dog. I reminded him to not interrupt Paddy or make eye contact because he was doing extremely well, calmly lying beside me. Each time he looked under the table, Paddy excitedly got up, wanting to go to him. I then had to resettle him again and again beside me. After several attempts to get his dog to come to him, I stood up, clapped my hands and said, "Hey," abruptly and with authority. I reiterated my request for him to ignore his dog, which he finally did.

This is the exact same method I would have used to correct Paddy if he continued to misbehave. It was obvious that Steven was the softie in the house. He just wanted to play with his dog. It just happened to be the wrong time to play. I was forced to control both ends of the situation. The dog was the easy part; it was the owner who was the pain in the neck.

Sometimes it is not enough to have control over your dog when you come across another dog and owner. Often dog owners feel it is appropriate for their dog to approach without asking if you are OK with it. This is when you need to assert yourself. I find that the best thing is put my hand up to indicate *stop* and then say, "My dog is in training. Please keep your dog back … thank you." People are usually very respectful of a dog in training, as they understand the importance.

You must, therefore, always be in control of the whole situation, even if you must raise your voice at another dog and/or dog owner. Never take *no* for an answer. Unfortunately, sometimes you need to be firmly proactive.

# Part 2

# Dog Park Lessons

## Dog Park Custodian

*Someone has to do it.*

**A Note to My Readers**

In this part of the book, I fictitiously take on the identity of Brewster, my nick name, part-time dog park custodian who volunteers at a local leash-free dog park. I use this character to address a collection of misbehaviors through dog park guests. Most of the visitors only know me as Brewster, The Dog Park Guy, while others know my identity as the dog whisperer. Brewster often says things or uses quotes that Bruce the dog whisperer would use. Of course, I always have Satchmo, my work partner and best friend, with me. I work on Sunday mornings, cleaning up the park and doing odd jobs to keep the place orderly.

I routinely mingle with a variety of visiting owners and their dogs. If an owner is having a problem with their dog(s), I offer my support. Each week brings a lesson on how to overcome a specific misbehavior. My mission is to teach dog owners the *canine way* and how to think like dogs.

This is a game-changer for the owners, i.e., to be able to look at the world through their dog's eyes. After each dog park lesson, I've included a related real-life dog whisperer story from my practice. At the end of every chapter there is a summary, which can be used as a future quick reference regarding specific misbehaviors.

## **Chapter 17**

## **The Golden Rule – The No. 1 Rule**

*Tell them once and never take no for an answer.*

The sun was coming up as I arrived at the dog park one very hot Sunday morning in August. I was surprised to be met by a middle-aged couple in the parking lot. I looked at my watch; it was not quite 6:30 a.m. In the summer, I usually get to the park bright and early to beat the heat. Working here is my *volunteer job*, and I don't promote my dog-whispering services. I only work on Sunday mornings, as this allows me to contribute my time to a worthy cause.

It was unusual for someone to get to the park earlier than me. The couple seemed to be waiting for me by their car. I was hardly out of my own when they approached and asked if my name was Brewster. It seemed my reputation had preceded me. (Dog owners are like mothers who get talking in the schoolyard – word gets around.) I stuck out my hand and said, "Good morning." They introduced themselves as Wendy and Zan. Their stunning three-year-old Hungarian Vizsla's name was Chance.

Vizslas happen to be one of my favorite breeds. They are incredibly smart, handsome, have tons of energy and they love the water. Although not an overly common breed in North America, they are the national dog of Hungary, they are becoming better known because they make great family pets. Their abundance of energy can be a problem for owners who are not overly active. This breed needs an inordinate amount of exercise.

As we walked toward the park gate, it took everything Satchmo had to contain his excitement. I had to give him a couple of 'Hey' sounds to keep him in check. He was dying to meet Chance, who was pulling, jumping and bouncing like a Super Ball without any correction whatsoever from either Wendy or Zan. As soon as we entered the park, they released Chance off her leash, so I gave Satchmo the OK to take off. Clearly, they couldn't wait to let Chance go, as she seemed to be more of a nuisance than a pleasure to be with.

It was obvious that they hadn't done much research on choosing the best breed for their lifestyle. Matching energy levels should be the first and foremost consideration when choosing a breed. Viszlas are super smart and love obedience training; in fact, they thrive on it. Chance on the other hand was totally unruly. It was evident that they hadn't done any obedience training.

Wendy, Zan and I sat on the bench to chat; and they let forth a barrage of complaints about Chance. She wouldn't come when called; pulled like a wild dog when walking down the street; barked incessantly when the doorbell rang; and jumped on everyone she met. The list went on and on. Wendy and Zan stopped complaining just long enough for me to ask if they had done any obedience training with Chance. I was surprised to hear they had taken her to a novice obedience class. "She failed the course," they told me. I asked if the instructors had handled her or if they had been the handlers. They told me that the instructors never handled her at all.

Next, I asked if the instructors had talked to them or to Chance. The answer was, of course, that the instructors spoke only to them. I asked, "If the instructors only talked to you guys and you were the only ones handling Chance, then who really failed the course?" There were a few seconds of silence as this was an 'aha' moment. Suddenly the focus was off Chance and on them. I repeated my question. "Who failed the course?" They both nodded their heads slowly as they agreed that *they* had failed the obedience class, not Chance.

"I would put the intelligence level of a Vizsla in the top 10 breeds," I said. If they put the time into training her, she had the ability to be a super dog, rather than the uncontrollable brat that she was. Her potential was unbelievable.

At the time that Chance came into their lives, they had been extremely busy, and Chance wasn't their priority. Wendy's mother had suddenly become ill and all of their time had been directed to her recovery.

If Wendy and Zan wanted a well-behaved and well-rounded dog, it was going to take a significant amount of effort. "The louder you yell," I said, "the bigger the echo. Bigger effort gets better results."

I believe that obedience training is mandatory with every dog, as it naturally creates pack balance, along with respect from a dog. I shared with them that I'd owned a Vizsla many years ago, so I had first-hand experience with their exuberance. She was a very special companion in my life, never to be forgotten.

At this point in our conversation, Chance came running over to us, accompanied by another dog, also an early riser. It looked like an unkept Doodle. Both dogs wanted some human interaction and started to jump on Wendy and Zan, with their dirty paws. Both Wendy and Zan yelled several times at Chance: "Get off, get off." but to no avail. I stood up, clapped my hands, stepped toward them and sharply said, "Hey." Both dogs immediately got off and calmly looked up at me. I sat down, waited for a few seconds and then tapped my thigh, indicating that I wanted them to come to me. They both approached calmly and respectfully as I put my hands out to give them both a rub of praise for coming to me.

Wendy and Zan's yelling expressed their anger and frustration, but the dogs read this as weakness, not strength. I pointed away, indicating for the dogs to leave us, and they suddenly took off to continue their play. Somewhat astonished, Zan said, "I have no idea how you just did that, but it was certainly effective. Does it come in pill form?"

I laughed; "I have voodoo dust on my shoes that gives me great power."

Wendy, also bewildered, asked, "How the heck did you do that? Both dogs stopped jumping immediately and calmly approached you with just the tap of your hand. Next you pointed away from us and they took off. Are you Dr. Doolittle?"

"Hardly," I said. I explained that saying, "Hey," sharply, clapping my hands and standing up interrupted the dogs and redirected their focus to me. By standing and stepping forward, I physically increased my presence. They immediately jumped down and showed respect, as they lowered their heads slightly, put their ears back and lowered their tails, which had previously been straight up. I then gave them a common hand signal to come to me by tapping my leg. After I praised them for doing what I wanted, I then pointed away for them to leave us. Other than a chimpanzee, I believe that a dog is the only other animal that will follow the direction that we point. Don't waste your time pointing with a cat. I also mentioned that I didn't get angry, upset or yell. I always had calm strong energy.

I suggested that Wendy and Zan sign up for another obedience course in September, when classes started up again. Fortunately, this was only a few weeks away. In the meantime, I gave them a couple of basic training tips to focus on. The first concept I introduced was the Golden Rule: *"Tell them once and never take no for an answer."* The title alone indicates how significant this rule is. No other rule comes before it in the Game of Canine. I first came up with this rule when I was in my twenties; when I started training dogs, and I haven't changed it since.

Most people tend to repeat a command when giving it to a dog. By repeating a command, we dilute its importance. Imagine an army general giving an order to a private: "Private, guard the door and don't let anyone in." Would the general repeat the command several times, or would he expect the private to do exactly what he was told after giving the order the first time? We know the answer to that one. If the private didn't obey the order immediately, the general would call the military police and have the private removed.

"Tell Chance what you want her to do *once* and *never* take *no* for an answer," I said. "It's an order, Private Chance. Canines have a military mindset so repeating the command would only dilute the order given and diminish the rank of the person giving the order."

An alpha in the canine world would never take *no* for an answer. He would give a hard stare or a growl or viciously attack a disobedient pack member. I suggested that Wendy and Zan get out the book of lessons that they had received from the obedience classes that *they* had failed; so that they could review and practice the lessons they'd been taught. The difference this time should be that they would bring much more vigor to the task. "If you work on your lessons with the Golden Rule in mind, Chance will exponentially become a very obedient dog," I said.

I also suggested that they practice their obedience commands, with extra focus on *recall,* or *come* command. Call her name to get her attention, say, "Come," and add a hand signal of your choice (I use my right hand touching my left shoulder). You could include a slight tug on the leash at the same time, which will give her a triple message; voice, hand signal and a tug of the leash. Remember to give huge praise when she comes. This would be an ideal time for a treat."

"I suggest that you always praise her by petting her before you give her a treat. This will give her two forms of reward. If you don't have a treat handy, you can always give her a touch or physical praise alone, which should always be the primary form of reward. By repeating this process over and over and over, it will become automatic for her to come when called, since you consistently praise and treat her.

Keep in mind the Golden Rule. This premise is the same for all commands. At first focus on and master these three commands: come, sit and stay. Dog-time is slower than human-time, so be patient, slow down, keep calm. As odd as this may sound, the slower you progress, the faster she will learn. Progressing too quickly will take you one step forward and two steps backward. Master each step until it becomes solid and boring for her before going on to the next step. This will ensure steadfast progress.

I felt that I had given Wendy and Zan a lot to process (the Golden Rule, focus on calm, strong energy and lots of obedience commands, adding hand signals). I suggested that they go home, write down what we talked about and study the obedience lessons from their previous classes. This would give them lots to work on before they started classes again in a few weeks. I look forward to seeing them all at the park in the future, when their combo-pack is in better balance.

**Dog Whisperer Story; the Nightmare Cocker Spaniel**

To my astonishment, late one February evening, just before my bedtime, the phone rang. It was Irene, a widowed senior who owned two dogs, a Labrador Retriever and a Cocker Spaniel, calling me with a Mayday cry for help. Hunter, the Lab, was quite elderly and had been a treat to live with for more than fourteen years. The Cocker Spaniel was about a year old, and she was a nightmare. Her name was Speckles, named for the million spots or little specks all over her. Hunter was completely deaf and almost totally blind. He still went to the door when he wanted out, had enough energy to go for short walks and greeted people with the proverbial wagging tail of a Lab. He was a dog in his very senior years who had been an ideal family member in good standing since the day he arrived in their home. The only thing that one could ask for regarding Hunter, is that he live for another fourteen years.

Irene had become a widow only about four months previous. Her husband, Art, considered Speckles his dog, while Hunter was always the family dog. The two of them spent most of the day together. A retired accountant, Art kept himself busy with friends, lots of walking and was generally always on the go. He and Speckles were inseparable. After Art died very suddenly, Irene was forced into the role of what she described as a 'dog mother'.

After a couple of months of putting up with Speckles' mischievous behavior, Irene considered finding a new home for her. She felt that it might be better for the dog, as she was still quite young, and another family could provide a better life for her. The weeks passed, and Speckles' behavior got worse and worse, to the point that she was biting Irene. One day, while in a fit of anger, Irene put her in the car and drove to the local SPCA. As she pulled into the parking lot, her angst turned into compassion and she immediately did a U-turn and headed back home. She later told me, "Art would roll over in his grave if I gave her up." Later that night she found my name on the internet and made the Mayday call to me.

Irene told me about how Speckles wouldn't listen to her; she tugged her down the street when walking, growled and snarled when she tried to put her in the crate at night. She also mentioned that her biting had progressed to a point of drawing blood several times.

I agreed to meet and see what I could do to help. As I approached Irene's house I heard a dog barking intensely. I guessed that Speckles was barking due to her leadership mindset and she was protecting her pack. I, of course, never know what I'm going to encounter. Speckles was standing in front of Irene and in a very excited state. Irene was holding her back by the collar. I asked her to let Speckles go.

The dog came at me like she'd been shot from a cannon, with uncontrollable, explosive energy. I instantly put on my slip lead, gave it a gentle pop, said, "Hey," and put my hands above her. Along with my calm, strong, green-ring energy this was enough to park her in a sit position. She was still wiggling but she was showing respect.

Irene said to me, "That's the same control Art used to have with her."

I responded, "It just goes to show you that she knows what to do, and therefore my job is to teach you how to get the same results."

She then laughed: "Who do I make the check out to? I can't believe this is my dog."

All the while this was going on, Hunter was barking non-stop. It was not Speckles, it had been Hunter making all the commotion while he was tethered to his crate. I asked Irene to release him, so he could come to me. As soon as he reached me, I touched the back of his neck with a very slight squeeze. (His mother used to put her mouth over the back of his neck the same way.) He instantly stopped barking and gave me the once-over, using his nose.

Smell is a dog's primary sense, the only sense that dogs are born with. Hunter's sniffer was working just fine. Amazingly, even though he couldn't have heard me, he sensed me well before I stepped onto the porch. This shows the power of a canine's sensitivity to energy. He knew that I was approaching well before Speckles or Irene by utilizing this innate powerful skill. His barking began well before I rang the doorbell to warn Irene of my presence and persisted when I was in the house, because he wanted off the leash, so he could come and meet me. Once I touched him, he relaxed and accepted the new pack pecking order. Irene's constant nattering to him, in her attempt to quiet him, was all to no avail.

I introduced some fundamentals to the Game of Canine along with the idea of the Golden Rule to Irene: *"Tell Speckles once and never take no for an answer."* I brought to her attention how many times she gave both dogs various commands. She was not successful in keeping Hunter quiet by continuously telling him to stop barking, nor was she able to settle Speckles when I arrived. She repeated the same words over and over, telling Speckles to settle down.

"Remember when you said that I had the same control over her as Art did? Did Art or I take *no* for an answer? This is the most important rule in the Game of Canine and is definitely a black or white rule.

Hunter and Speckles respectfully remained calm throughout my visit, as I taught my lessons about how to play the Game of Canine. Irene was on an emotional mission to overcome Speckles' negative behavior, out of respect for her late husband. The idea of finding her a new home dissipated as she watched her dog become balanced.

On my second visit, once again, the only dog that I heard at the door was Mr. Hunter. As soon as I entered, I approached him, gave him a gentle touch, and he quietly lay down to relax. Speckles was controlling herself, albeit amply exited, but she was a total treasure at that moment. Irene was beaming with pride over her new balanced and very respectful behavior. The Golden Rule had worked. Walks with Speckles were now a pleasure; she went in and out of her crate calmly and there was absolutely no biting. All this was music to my ears; another victory in the world of dog whispering.

"I love it when a plan comes together."

It was now up to Irene to be a consistent leader and keep Speckles in balance forever.

## The *Gray* Smidgen Effect

*Black or white to the nth degree.*

Because of our tendency as humans, to be *gray* when dealing with dogs, we must constantly focus on living in their black or white world. Each time we play 'just a little gray' and not 100 percent leader (black), we give up a smidgen of leadership. One smidgen plus one smidgen plus one smidgen can add up quickly. A smidgen to us is so small that typically we don't even notice it. Even if we do recognize a tiny slip-up, we immediately forget about it. But smidgens, as small as we perceive them to be, become an issue of posturing in the pecking order. This is exactly what we are trying to avoid, i.e., forcing a dog to take the dominant leader position.

It's very easy to give up smidgens of leadership. For example:

1. You gave your dog a sit/stay command as you answered your door. While you were talking with the person at the door, he walked over to your visitor, who gave him some rubs. You realized, at that point, that he had broken his sit/stay command. However, you let it go because you didn't want to correct him in front of someone else.

2. You arrived home in your car with your dog. As you were getting out of the car you gave him a sit/stay command while you gathered up your things. He sat brilliantly for about 30 seconds. A split second before you were about to give him a 'come' command, he jumped out of the car on his own. You said to yourself, "Close enough. I was about to call him out anyway." But he made the decision to jump out of the car, not you.

In both examples, your dog broke your command, and you broke the Golden Rule; *You took no for an answer.* Sometimes a misbehavior seems petty or unimportant to us, so we let it go and forget about it. A gray smidgen here and there compound in his world, and contribute to your dog's dominant ranking mindset, which nurtures misbehaviors. The rules to the Game of Canine are distinctly black or white; there's no in between, not even a smidgen.

In both examples above it would be prudent to re-set the dog's position with a sit/stay command and make them obey the order. This investment of time and effort will pay off with future commands.

**Summary**

Dogs and kids are very much alike. They can be naughty or good but generally they want to be good. When dogs step out of line, which they are programmed to do, it is an opportunity to teach them a positive lesson, followed by praising them and giving a treat. If they get away with the negative behavior, they are certain to repeat their actions. Of course, the mission is to teach them to live within the rules. At any given time ask yourself, "Am I playing the *gray* Game of Human or the *black or white* Game of Canine?"

In the Game of Canine, dogs need, want and thrive on pack balance. Obedience training helps with this process. By starting obedience training at the puppy stage, problems tend not to develop. I believe that all dogs need basic obedience training. Remember that the student at obedience classes is the dog owner, not the dog. Once you learn how to train your dog, it is up to *you* to pass the lessons on to your best friend.

Mastering a couple of key issues when training will make the process that much more effective and rewarding;

1. Live by the Golden Rule.

2. Always focus on emitting calm, strong, green-ring, leader-energy. Dogs are super-sensitive at reading energy – you can't fool them. You must be a calm dog owner to have a calm dog.

# Chapter 18

## Dog-to-Dog Aggression

*Be cognizant and avoid problems.*

Early one morning, while in deep thought clearing the fence line with an electric trimmer, a stranger startled the heck out of me. “Brewster.” he yelled over the noise of the trimmer. He approached and introduce himself as Jim. His friend Emily had told him that I was always at the park Sunday mornings.

Jim’s dog, Corbett, was feverishly running with all the dogs with the usual excitement and boundless energy one would expect from a Jack Russell Terrier. All seemed quite normal and fun until Corbett came over to where we were standing, for a break in play, and lay beside Jim, as if to say, “I’ve had enough!” Jim put on his leash to indicate that playtime was over. As a Pug came close to try and entice Corbett back into play, Corbett instantly went into a rage; barking, snarling and lunging at the pug, the very dog he’d been playing with a few seconds before.

Jim tried to get control with no luck whatsoever. It was only when the Pug decided to return to the other dogs that Corbett finally settled down. “Why is Corbett aggressive only when he’s on the leash?” asked Jim. I told him that Corbett was working and on-duty when he was close to him while leashed, but off-duty when free and wandering away from Jim.

“It is quite amazing how happy and playful he is when he’s not working,” said Jim. I agreed, as I had previously witnessed Corbett interacting with all the other dogs. As we were talking, the same Pug once again moved toward us to encourage Corbett to play some more. I suggested to Jim that he unleash Corbett. The two dogs immediately began to run and play together. I then asked Jim to call Corbett and re-leash him, which he did. The Pug was not far behind him as the two dogs approached us. Instantly, as if a switch had been turned on when Jim attached his leash, Corbett went into a rant of aggression toward the Pug, who did an about face and walked away. He then stopped and looked back over his shoulder as if to say, "You're weird."

When a dog is on-duty, he assumes a protector/dominant role, which is the leader's job. When off duty, he can simply be a dog playing at the park, which means he will fall into his position within the ranking of the park pack.

Therefore, when walking down the street with Jim, and on-duty from Corbett's point of view, he is always working. I suggested that Jim start thinking like-a-dog, so he could understand why Corbett acts as he does and why he feels the need to take on the protector's role. I also suggested that he try a different type of leash and collar. He was using a nylon leash, which is harsh on one's hands, along with a flat collar. Jim was a chiropractor, which meant he had soft sensitive hands. A flat collar is very common but offers no correction whatsoever when he gives the leash a pop for Corbett to refocus on him. The flat collar was also easy for Corbett to escape from; all he had to do was back out of it, because the size was static. Jim added, "He has escaped from this collar several times."

I told Jim, "I believe that you need a leash and collar system that will facilitate a correction whenever Corbett is misbehaving. I use a slip lead myself. This will allow you to set the snugness of the collar part of the system, and if either of you pulls on the leash, it will tighten. Hence, he will not be able to back out of it. This will take the process up a notch in terms of correcting him. The slip lead will give Corbett a very quick squeeze, then instantly relax and go loose.

The idea of a correctional pop or flick is to redirect his focus to you. When he starts to get fixated on another dog, you can easily redirect his focus with a light pop and at the same time change direction, which also redirects his focus as he has to turn and catch up to you. I would add the sound 'Hey' at the same time to accentuate your message.

We walked over to my car so that I could show him a slip lead and we put the slip lead on Corbett. He was quite responsive as Jim walked him across the parking lot, with no apprehension whatsoever.

Note: Dog-on-dog aggression can be caused by a multitude of reasons besides on-duty dominance. When puppies are taken from their litter too early, the lack of social interaction with their siblings can ultimately lead to unsociable, aggressive behavior. The same aggression can also be caused by a dog being attacked by another dog earlier in life, for example in a shelter before adoption. The new owner would be completely mystified as to why their new dog was aggressive. An early attack can cause a dog to be overly offensive or aggressive, in an insecure way, to thwart off any potential problems. This is known as fear-aggression. Another frustrating reason is the nature of the dog's gene pool, which may cause a bully-effect.

I told Jim, "The fundamental cure for this problem is to strongly fill the role of the leader, so that Corbett can be a non-working off-duty dog at all times. You need to control every situation." I added, "It doesn't matter what the reason is for Corbett's aggression – you must give him the confidence that *you* will protect *him* from all evil threats."

I suggested that he try to get control of Corbett a good distance away from other dogs before getting too close. Even walking on the other side of the street could create a situation. I said, "Think of a dart board. You want to get control in the outer ring before you progressively move into the intensity of the bull's-eye. You can try this at a park or anywhere else that people walk their dogs. If this is done a good distance away, say the opposite end of the park, the threat level should be at a minimum, facilitating a higher level of success. When that distance is manageable, then try to move him in closer and closer, until you get within a comfortable distance of other dogs."

Corbett does not have to meet every dog he encounters; just as we don't shake hands and talk to every person we see. I am frequently mystified that many dog owners believe that it is their dog's *right* to be able to approach every dog they come across.

I told Jim that when Corbett begins barking and showing his nasty side, try stepping in front of Corbett. "Get into his face or space so that he *feels* your presence, with your shins touching his nose. Then continue to shuffle into his space until he moves back. Initiate this by saying, "Hey," and clap your hands to get his attention. Also, learn to proactively anticipate when he is about to ramp up his focus and try to physically redirect him beforehand.

"This would be a good time to hold up a dog treat to divert his attention from another dog and back to you. This may not be overly effective, as dogs won't eat when stressed. You could also put your hand under his chin so that he keeps focusing on you and the treat. Another option is to change directions as you walk away while holding a treat. Corbett needs to know the distinct difference of negative and positive actions. When he gives up his aggression and redirects his focus to you, show him a ton of praise. Your vocal praise should be accompanied by your lavishly petting him along with giving him the treat. This will encourage repetitive positive behavior."

A total victory for Jim and his dog would be for Corbett to be able to pass other dogs on the street and not react negatively. I told Jim, "Keep things in proportion. Don't expect him to not even look at the other dog. Looking is 'free' as long as he does not show signs of moving forward. It will take lots of practice to keep Corbett in balance and off-duty while on a leash. Like most things, practice makes perfect. This is not a quick fix but a *process* for you both to master. Change in dog behavior is progressive, be it good or bad."

Ideally Jim wanted to expunge Corbett's entire dog-on-dog aggression. I mentioned to him that if he wanted total success and to be able to get close enough for Corbett to meet other dogs, it was important for him to proceed with unhurried caution and to be very selective in his choice of dogs for Corbett to meet and greet. I said,

“Pick a balanced dog, not one showing fear or overly dominant. A female would be the best choice.

Start the meeting process from a distance that you feel comfortable with. Watch both dogs intently and be patient. If they are fixated on each other, this indicates that you should *not* move forward with the meeting. Both dogs must be calm and not focused with a hard stare. If they are using their nose and sniffing toward the other, this is ideal because smelling shows curiosity. If all remains calm, keep cutting the distance in half.”

I cautioned Jim, “Please do not hesitate to stop the process at any point. It would be a win if Corbett remained in a calm state up until then. You should also be evaluating both the other dog and owner. If they are showing signs of nervousness or concern, a red flag should go up – for *stop*.” There is no time limit on this and remember that dog-time is slower than human-time. At this point the two dogs will likely be only a few feet apart. The key is that both dogs are containing themselves. They may be calm or excited, with tails wagging, but are respective of their owners.

"Wait until you feel that all dogs and owners are exhibiting balanced energy. Maybe the dogs are showing signs of excitement and want to play, e.g., a play-bow or a quick movement with a smile on their face. This would be an ideal scenario but stay focused and do not misread this. Often a slow, swishing tail is mistaken for one of high speed that wiggles the whole back end of the dog – the latter is friendly, the former is not. The worst tail is when it is puffed up and on a 45-degree angle with several curves in it. This angle is a serious warning sign that aggression is about to take place. Anticipate this by being cognizant of the whole situation.

The last step is to let them meet while you stay highly focused on both dogs. Read their body language for any changes, e.g., hackles raised; putting their head or legs over top of the other dog; humping; continued stare in a face to face stance; or any sounds of growling whatsoever. Canines can growl at a decibel level that humans are unable to hear, so if you are hearing a growl it has likely been going on longer than you realize. Keep your leash loose, not fully lying on the ground, just absent of tension. Also watch the other owner's leash to see what message he or she is sending; it is either calm or not."

"There's a lot to this isn't there Jim?" I said. "Ideally the dogs will smell each other head to tail. Let this happen without interruption unless something changes, as the main hurdle has been overcome and nature will take its course. If they show signs of playfulness, then let them play and be themselves for a short while. My suggestion is that you be the one to decide when it is time to stop and move on. Keep watch that one doesn't get overly dominant with the other. This will only escalate to a problem." It's like when children's play escalates and a parent steps in and says, "That's enough. Someone is going to get hurt."

"An important reminder is that this process will take time, not just a day or two but potentially much longer, depending on both the dog and owner. The biggest mistake you can make is to proceed too quickly, which will set you both back."

Jim said he was looking forward to practicing at the soccer pitch near his house, where there were lots of families with dogs. His plan was to start at the opposite side of the park to begin Corbett's new training regime.

I looked forward to positive updates from Jim on Corbett's future dog-park visits.

## Dog Whisperer Story; Luger, the hater of all dogs

I was called to a home with a Doberman Pinscher named Luger, who was extremely aggressive with other dogs. My experience with Luger is a heartwarming example of how an out-of-balance dog can change in very short order. By simply realigning Luger's pack position, I was able to help him change his job description from leader/protector to that of follower. Suddenly Luger was playing defense instead of offense.

Shortly after I had balanced Luger and taught Caroline, his owner, the rules to the Game of Canine, we all went outside their home for a short walk. Our timing was ideal because a young mother with a stroller and a Weimaraner were walking past on the other side of the street. This was the perfect scenario to test Luger. I called out across the street and asked the neighbour if she would help us with Luger's training and simply stop and wait with her dog. She readily agreed.

The first approach I made was to stop and maintain a calm with Luger from afar, at the end of Caroline's driveway. Next, I moved to the middle of the street and stopped to ensure that Mr. Luger was still in his calm, follower mindset. He was indeed, so I continued to the other side of the street. It was a serious test for him to be within such close proximity to the young woman, her baby and her dog. Once again, he exhibited absolutely no aggression whatsoever. He wasn't even looking at the Weimaraner. I then proceeded to the bull's-eye of the potential storm, as we got within a few feet of the Weimaraner.

The whole time I didn't take my eyes off Luger, except for a quick glance at the woman and her dog to make sure they were OK. My focus on Luger was intense but calm. All was fine. Luger was in a submissive *sit* position with his weight on his rump. He was a perfect gentleman. Well done, Luger. I then thanked the woman for being an ideal distraction for him.

I returned Luger to Caroline back in her driveway, and gave him a ton of praise and rubs.

"I would have bet you my house that you couldn't have done that", she said.

I said, "I wouldn't want to see you homeless." I asked if she would like to try it herself. Caroline declined because she didn't feel confident enough. She was, however, blown away to see her dog behave so calmly with absolutely no aggression whatsoever, the Luger of her dreams.

To be able to show people their dog's full potential, simply because of balance, is very special. Even though it is the exact behavior that I envision and expect, I am always pleased and impressed with how quickly and radically a dog can change.

Luger's story shows how dogs are reactors. They react to me when I arrive. They know instantly that I am a leader with calm, strong, green-ring leader-energy with no aggression toward them. They also sense that I am there to take over the pack. They either accept this or reject me, which means we fight. Of course, my mandate is to win, using my mind, and not have to fight. It is rare to see dogs engage in a battle, because they typically don't want the leader's job.

Luger was more than happy to give up his pack position. Caroline was motivated because she saw what Luger was capable of. She was fully engaged into her new mission to keep Luger balanced and to progress to where she was confident that Luger would not get into dog fights because he felt it was his job to protect her.

For Caroline's confidence to grow, I suggested a cage muzzle, which would not be offensive to Luger. The muzzle is a people-tool because it helps an owner like Caroline remain calm and confident that her dog cannot hurt another dog or person, which empowers her to position herself high on her Leader Ladder.

Caroline made astounding progress during the week between visits. Whenever she and Luger were out walking across the street from other dogs, Luger remained calm. This was tremendous progress for both of them, and in only one week.

During our second session, I brought along my special working partner, Mr. Satchmo. This is where he is at his best. The mission was to introduce Luger and Satchmo and let them smell and touch each other, hopefully with play in mind, from Luger's point of view. If Luger only tolerated Satchmo, without aggression, we'd declare it a victory.

Caroline asked if I would handle Luger while I opened the tailgate to my car. (Satchmo simply waits calmly and adapts to a situation in the presence of another dog.) Luger was the ideal gentleman as we approached Satchmo. They were close enough to sniff each other and touch noses. Next it was Caroline's turn to handle Luger. I leashed Satchmo and brought him out of the car. If there was going to be an incident it would probably happen when Caroline was handling Luger, as she was not yet to the top of her Leader Ladder. Therefore, a victory would be for her to keep Luger calm a short distance away from Satchmo and not push her luck by getting too close. My concern was that this would push Caroline backward a couple of steps. The mission was to win in the end. I told her not worry about how long it took.

Caroline was totally successful with Luger from the width of her double driveway away from Satchmo, then about half the distance, and finally half the distance again. She considered this to be a monumental victory.

We then traded dogs with the intent to get Luger and Satchmo to play together. With both dogs in a balanced state, this presented the best opportunity for Luger's success. At first Luger was a little tentative but very quickly he put his elbows on the ground and his bum in the air as if to say, "Let's play." We let the two of them run around for a little while and then re-leashed them. This playtime with Satchmo was almost unprecedented since it had been several years since Luger had played with another dog.

"I can't believe how simple this process has been", she said. "All I had to do was follow your Recipe and *voilà!* ... Speaking of recipes, I have an unbelievable recipe for sparerib sauce. Everyone raves about it? Would you like me to email it to you?"

Apologetically, I told her I was a vegetarian. We both laughed.

In our follow-up phone conversations, it was great to hear how well both Caroline and Luger were doing. They are now able to walk past dogs on the *same* side of the street. She also mentioned that they both had lower blood pressure.

**Summary**

Aggression toward other dogs, while a dog is on a leash, indicates that he is in a working or dominant mode and therefore feels obligated to protect his owner. Often insecure dogs are forced into the dominant protective role, causing fear-aggression. Both can be cured by the same method; calm, strong leadership. This gives dogs confidence because they know their leader will protect them and not the reverse.

To change the mind or behavior of a dog, you must take a proactive leadership approach. First master managing your dog from a distance before progressively getting closer. If you cannot maintain a calm dog from halfway across the park, then move farther back. It is mandatory that your dog remains calm. Maintain this mindset as you continue to move closer and closer over time. Don't move toward the bull's-eye too quickly. The results will hinge on how high your dog perceives you to be on your Leader Ladder.

*Control the calm to win the game!* Always be proactive and keep an eye open for other dogs.

# Chapter 19

## Five Ways to Communicate in Canine

*"Seek first to understand, then to be understood." – Stephen R. Covey*

Some days the commotion at the dog park can be annoying. The noise made by the dogs is not an issue. In fact, I love the sound of dogs playing, running, panting, barking, drinking and splashing in the creek. It reminds me of the happy, natural sounds of kids playing in a schoolyard. It is the yelling and screaming by the dog owners that I find frustrating. Some people seem to think that dogs can speak our language, whether it is English, French, Spanish or any other language, for that matter. They must believe this with all their hearts; otherwise why would they continuously yell at their dogs?

One Sunday, while I was cleaning up poop, I counted as a man called his Soft Coated Wheaten Terrier to come, 16 times. "Jack come. Jack come here. I'm not going to tell you again, Jack, Jack get over here. Jack, Jack, Jack ..." His voice got louder and louder. The yelling went on *ad nauseam.* His volume was all over the place, from calling to screaming, as his irritation level approaching insanity. All the time Jack turned a deaf ear. Eventually he wandered back to his owner, but only after satisfying his need to snoop around. It was *he* who decided when it was time to go home.

This brings up my favorite question; "When did I give up control?" It would be hard for this owner to give up something he'd never had.

Jokingly, I often ask dog owners how many words their dog has spoken to them. They all give the answer; "None." So why do most people keep talking to dogs and expect them to understand a 10-word sentence?

Words are our number one way to communicate; *not theirs*.

If you speak to your dog using one or two-word sentences only, and these words are ones that you use repeatedly, there is a much better likelihood that your dog will receive your message. In my experience there are five distinct levels of communication with dogs. *Words* are No. 5, the lowest level. In descending order, these are the five levels of canine communication:

**1. Energy**

Dogs use this amongst themselves and have a unique ability to read or sense energy from all animals, including humans, from a significant distance. The canine's survival technique is to sense danger, even when they can't see their enemy. Most owners can cite an example of their dog sensing something before it was revealed to them. Humans don't have this uncanny skill. We need to see someone to read their energy. Just as dogs can smell at a level we can't relate to, they can sense us well beyond our comprehension using this Superman-like ability. By understanding and respecting this strength, we exponentially increase our communication effectiveness.

Dogs can read-us-like-a-book. The question is not if we are sending a message but what is the message we are sending. By being cognizant of their super sensitive radar system, we can effectively communicate by controlling our energy, which reflects a myriad of emotions, e.g., anger, fear, frustration, embarrassment, excitement, sadness or green-ring calm. Which emotion is it?

To build our relationship with our dogs we must try to be continuously in a calm, strong state. Calm, strong, green-ring leader-energy builds respect, while other emotions vacate the leader's position, which automatically forces a dog to take on the leader's role. Either we have green-ring energy, or we don't. By using our higher level of intelligence, we can detect when we don't have green-ring, leader-energy. If we take couple of deep breaths, we can quickly relax and regain our calm leader-energy, reverting our mood-ring back to green. It is a major mistake to underestimate this primal form of canine communication.

**2. Body language**

Canines utilize many body parts to express themselves. For example, they use their tail as a major communicator; change their ears; eyes; mouth; raise their hackles; lean forward with weight on their front feet; as well as raise one foot. Each of these body parts explicitly sends a message to other canines.

There are a number of basic physical ways to connect with your dog and bring their focus to you. I often put my hand above a dog's head, palm down, without touching them. This creates a connection because they feel my energy. It's quite impacting. I also step into a dog's face/space, very close with my legs almost touching their nose, or shuffle into them to make them give up their space. Another example; lightly squeeze a dog's neck or pinch their scruff with a couple of fingers. Their redirected thoughts will automatically connect with you.

Eye contact or a stare is another simple, but strong physical form of connection. Try this exercise using body language with someone who happens to be sitting down. Start by standing an arm's length away from them. Make constant eye contact with the person. Don't break your stare and if possible don't blink. Next put your hand about six inches above them, toward the front of their head, so they know your hand is there. Finally, quickly step into their space. Get really close to them. The power of this exercise is quite significant. The person will feel your presence with far more impact than they expected, all due to body language.

**3. Leash**

A leash clearly has a direct connection to your dog. There is a constant flow of energy through the leash from you to your dog. The important question is whether the leash is loose or tight. If the leash is tight, the energy flow expresses nervousness, and your dog will feel obligated to protect you, as you are showing tension or weakness. A loose leash represents calm, green-ring energy.

It is amazing how simple, yet implicitly impactful, a leash can be. Far too often nervous dog owners walk their dog with a short, tight leash because they feel this gives them more control. Yet it has the exact opposite effect by forcing the dog into assuming the dominant protective position. The true leash is mental, via our energy. Become keenly aware of which message you are sending through your leash.

**4. Hand signals and whistles**

When a child is raised in a family with parents who speak multiple languages, they typically learn all the languages spoken in the home. Dogs are very similar, as they too can learn multiple ways to receive human communication. To teach a dog a command or trick requires repeating a single word for each command accompanied by a reward or treat, which will encourage the dog to repeat the process. To enhance communication, add a hand signal and/or whistle sound. By utilizing all three methods, individually or in any combination, you can exponentially increase the effectiveness of your communication.

Because canines read each other's physical expression of tail, ears, eyes and posture, they are experts at reading us physically as well. I like to tap into this natural skill of theirs, so I consider both hand signals and whistles to be a more potent method of communication than words.

I once purchased a puppy I named Jazz, one of my favorite music genres, whose fourteen-year-old grandfather was totally deaf. The breeder said to me, "I wish that I'd taught him hand signals when he was younger, because he can't hear anything at this point". I took that statement to heart, and when I trained my pup I not only gave her voice commands but also hand signals and whistle sounds. It was effortless, teaching her all commands this way, and she became an extremely obedient dog. (Often, when at obedience trials, I'd used hand signals instead of voice commands when all the other competitors were talking to their dogs. I didn't realize at the time that I was using a more compelling form of communication.) Thank goodness that I taught my pup hand signals because at about age thirteen, she also went deaf. This handicap was minimized because I could still effectively communicate with her.

Many dogs go either deaf or blind in old age. By utilizing both audio and visual commands, communication with your pet can be maintained without much ado if either sense is lost. Most people didn't realize my dog was deaf, because we connected so well.

My dad was an amazing whistler and he taught me to whistle at a young age. It was natural for me then to add whistle sounds when dog training.

When Satchmo is at the park and a good distance away from me, I use both a hand signal and a whistle command. If he is not looking my way, he will still hear me whistle. If he is looking at me but my lips are dry, and my whistle isn't very strong, he will see my hand signal. When I am close to him, my whistle is very soft. It is all air with very little sound, like a whispering whistle.

It's prudent for all dog owners to master the five basic commands: come, sit, stay, down and heel. Practice giving each command with a word, hand signal and a whistle sound, if you can whistle. There is no universal list of hand signals or whistles. I use the following hand signals:

**Come:** I move my right hand across my chest and tap my left shoulder.

**Sit:** I raise my open hand, palm up, bending at the elbow like I'm doing a curl with weights.

**Stay:** With an open palm, I sharply move my hand in front of the dog's face.

**Down:** I point to the floor.

**Heel:** I make a quick hand motion around and behind my leg.

Any repeated, consistent motion will suffice for all these commands. There is a plethora of additional commands that can also be taught using hand signals/whistle sounds.

**5. Words**

Although dogs don't speak our language, they are quite capable of learning some of our words through repetition. Therefore, you should minimize the number of words in a sentence to succinctly get your message across to them. Use a single word for the basic commands (come, sit, stay, down, heel) and build your pet's repertoire from there. Dogs can build a significant vocabulary of single-word or short-sentence phrases. In some rare situations, dogs have been known to understand and respond to hundreds of words.

Always think of communication from the *canine* point of view, not human. I talk to Satchmo when we are wrestling. When I am hugging him, I say, "I love you", or I tell him how special he is and how proud I am of him. Typically, whenever I give Satchmo a verbal command, I whisper very softly. Someone standing only a short distance away would likely not hear me. (This is truly the only time that I actually whisper to dogs, even though I am a dog whisperer.) When you whisper to a dog, he must pay close attention to you. If you are always speaking loudly to him, this is much less effective, because he doesn't have to be as attentive. Just like children, dogs tune you out.

The only time I raise my voice is if a situation becomes serious. Say Satchmo and I are at our local park, while he's off leash and wandering across the parking lot, when a car rapidly approaches. It would be imperative that Satchmo immediately stop where he is. I am likely to whistle a quick, loud, 'Sit' command to get his attention as I briskly raise my hand for him to sit, accompanied by a sharp, harsh voice command. All three methods of communication would be utilized. When the situation is serious, and my commands need to be immediately and definitively received by Satchmo, the intensity of my communication increases exponentially.

Whenever I communicate to him at this extreme level, he instantly sits and fixates on me as he waits for his next command. When things are safe, I usually call him to me and give him praise and a rub for his stellar obedience, which could very well have saved his life. The ultimate obedience is for a dog to obey commands when off leash while being distracted by something or someone.

Teaching your dog multiple languages will augment your communication and connection with him. I often ask new clients to refrain from talking to their dog for several days or even a week. The goal is to encourage them to focus on the other four more effective ways to communicate with their dog; energy, body language, loose leash, and hand signals/whistles. On my second visit I ask them how it went. I typically get a variety of answers. Some say, "It was ridiculous, we couldn't do it". These folks got nothing out of this important exercise. Others say that they weren't perfect and succeeded maybe half the time, but they became distinctly aware of how much more they connected with their dog. Those who are the most successful at not talking to their dog, recognize how much more effective their communication became. They experience a new level of connection that they never imagined possible, oddly to them, because they stopped talking. This is a terrific exercise that is well worth giving a try.

**Try this; hug and kiss your dog as you tell him how much you love him. Next, wait a few seconds and try doing the exact same hug and kiss without talking. You will find that his response is no different than when you talked to him.**

**Our energy is more important than words.**

**Dog Whisperer Story; a blind rescue Collie**

A young couple who owned a blind collie asked me if I could help with her aggression. Willow was a northern First Nation rescue dog who had gone blind. Of course, the immediate reaction of most people would be to feel sorry for her. But would another dog meeting Willow feel sorry for her or just accept her for who she was? My mission is to think like a canine and not an emotional human. My focus was solely on balancing Willow and then teaching her owners, Dave and Sandi, how to maintain her balance as well as ways to communicate with her.

As I first entered their apartment, Willow was leashed and calmly sitting a short distance from the front door. As I bent over to untie my shoes, Willow aggressively lunged at me. I instantly stood up and took the leash from Dave. Then I got-in-her-face and showed her that I wasn't going to back off, as most people did. I posed no threat and showed no aggression or fear whatsoever. She innately sensed my green-ring energy and ultimately accepted me as the new leader of her pack. As usual no words had been spoken. Willow knew the pack dynamic had just changed.

We all sat down in the living room. Willow came over to me and put her forehead against the inside of my left knee. This was her way of showing total surrender to me: ears back, tail down and head lowered. Dave and Sandi had never seen Willow surrender to anyone. For her to show a new, submissive posture to me gave them hope.

Willow immediately lay beside me on her side in a prone position. This position expresses maximum calm for a dog. Any calmer and she'd be asleep. Normally, she was wary of guests, did not relax, and would position herself between Sandi and them, in other words, on-duty. All of this took place in only a few short minutes.

The immediate transformation from a dominant, confused mixed-up canine, to a totally submissive follower, always impresses me by the brevity of the process. This immediate pecking order realignment occurs because dogs are reactors to a change of circumstances. They don't have to analyze and figure things out. In fact they are unable to analyze things.

Even though Willow was blind, I wanted Dave and Sandi to concentrate on communicating with her without using words. This would force them to think about their emotional energy as well as focus on keeping a loose leash and using body language. Obviously, hand signals would be eliminated and replaced with various sounds, touches and whistle commands.

After I taught them The Recipe, or rules to the Game of Canine, we walked along the hallway in their apartment building to head outside for a brief walk. Willow walked beside me, close to the wall. As we approached a corner, she didn't miss a beat as she navigated her way around it. Her hearing was very acute, obviously a necessity for her. When we stepped outside near the parking lot at the rear of the building, I asked Dave and Sandi to wait by the back door. They would be outside her energy zone and would have no influence over her, especially if they were feeling their usual pity for her.

As I walked across the parking lot with Willow I varied my speed, from very slow to a short run and back to normal, then a quick walk, then super slow, then a run, etc., etc. I often changed directions with a quick about-face. Despite this erratic walking, I couldn't lose Willow. She stayed at my left side as if she was a champion in obedience, or we had Velcro stuck to both of us. No one would guess she had a visual handicap. Her leash was always loose. I was impressed by how well she 'tuned' into me.

Both Dave and Sandi were spellbound. We then walked out to the front of their building. This was literally Main Street, which had lots of traffic as well as a stoplight and a mall across the street. Willow would have plenty of variables to deal with.

I wanted to show Dave and Sandi some new ways to communicate with her. Since we didn't have to teach her to obediently walk on a leash, we could proceed to using sounds to communicate. I first mentioned that we needed to alert her when she was approaching a curb, otherwise she would hit and hurt her feet on the cement. A simple way to notify her, since she walked on the left side, would be for them to slide their left heel on the ground just before the curb, so that she would associate this sound with; *Curb up ahead.* Similarly, they could quickly drag their right heel to indicate; *Curb down ahead.* Additionally, they could also say, "Curb up," or "Curb down," to enhance the message. They needed to take advantage of her enhanced hearing.

The original reason they had called me was Willow's aggression toward humans. This became a non-issue. She was passing people on Main Street without any incident. When we went back into their building and walked through the lobby, where there were several people standing around, Willow was a perfect lady. The focus of her behavioral issues shifted to that of improving her life within her limitations of darkness. Happily, Willow's aggression issues had dissipated because of pack balance. Dave and Sandi would have to strictly follow The Recipe to maintain balance within their pack.

I suggested that the couple take turns walking around their building, both inside as well as outside, while one of them wore a blindfold. No cheating. The objective was for them both to understand and appreciate how critical it was to have explicit communication from the person acting as the guide when the other couldn't see anything. After all, Willow could only receive their communication via words, sounds or touches. This exercise was intended to help them develop empathy and understanding of her plight, not pity for her life of darkness. Willow's dependence on Dave and Sandi was obviously major.

Walking with a dog is the most important activity that we can participate in, as it builds both trust and respect. Dogs trust that their leader won't put them in harm's way and they respect their leader by following them wherever they are led. The goal of this exercise was to build compassion and respect, to show Sandi and Dave how essential their role is in acting as Willow's eyes. All three progressed beautifully with their newly realigned pack hierarchy.

I got a call about six months later, as Willow was regressing and starting to show some of her old aggression issues. As I listened to both Dave and Sandi telling me about the problems with Willow, I became aware of how competitive they were with each other. Both were exceptionally athletic and obviously had competed in various sports. As Sandi began to tell me how Dave had slacked off and not followed the rules to the Game of Canine, Dave would jump in to rat her out. This was quite uncomfortable for me, as this competitive flurry went back and forth in a game of, *he said, she said.*

I mentioned this constant dueling to them. They acknowledged that their competitive spirit was part of their attraction to each other. I suggested they think about it from Willow's viewpoint. How would she perceive this constant fighting between those who were supposed to be leaders she could respect and trust? The leadership of the pack was in a constant state of flux.

I said, "No wonder she is acting dominant and aggressive again. She feels forced into the position of leader because of arguing, which produces a void of leadership. She doesn't know what you are saying while you are in your debating mode, but she surely feels your turbulent energy. Canines cannot follow what they perceive to be instability. Leadership needs to be consistent, without fluctuations, not continuously inconsistent."

I added, "I suggest that you record some of your dueling conversations. Upon playing back the recording, you will hear the competitiveness in your voices. Even better, try listening to it with your eyes closed. This will heighten your other senses, allowing you to focus on your combative state."

I realized that they were not likely to change their style of communication with each other. Therefore, it would be even more important that they consciously follow The Recipe as closely as they possibly could, with distinct black or white on their minds. This would give them the best possible chance to keep balance in the pack. I asked if they would consider keeping their voice to a minimum when arguing in front of Willow, as well as adding some laughter if possible. This would at least minimize the level of negative energy perceived by her. Other than that, I knew they would not change their core personalities, nor would I expect them to. Their competitive nature was important and a natural attraction to each other.

In our next couple of conversations, I focused solely on their ability to play by the rules as closely as humanly possible. I felt that this was Willow's only hope. Nobody is perfect at the game, but Sandi and Dave's verbal jousting was certainly a cause of Willow's issues. Fortunately, they did become very efficient at the Game of Canine, and her aggressive behavior became quite manageable. It didn't drop to zero. It was close, but not perfect. They kept her in check by being extra cognizant when debating with each other. My guess is that they are still verbally arm wrestling, but all in all, this was another victory for pack balance.

## **Summary**

Canines and humans obviously communicate very differently. Our No. 1 way to express ourselves is through words, while their primary way is silent, through an expression of energy. By adjusting to their system, we can communicate with them very effectively.

When I was a young boy, my father brought home a television. It was truly incomprehensible that we could watch about six different shows on this magical machine. Understanding that the *rabbit ears* on top of the set could pick up the signal being transmitted through the air, was overwhelming to me. Of course, the shows were in black and white, as well as rather *snowy* in clarity. Compare this example of *ancient* 1950s technology, to modern-day electronics, which have the power to view shows or videos from around the world with incredible clarity and definition. In the world of human-canine communication, humans are like an old black-and-white TV set, while canines are like modern-day electronic devices with infinite power.

It is imperative that as humans we recognize and respect canines' superior command of reading our energy. When we understand this sensitivity, we can then become more effective communicators in the language of canine by controlling our messages. I know that my understanding of this fact is a strength, which allows me to send a message through my calm strong, green-ring energy. The question is not *if* we are sending a message but *what* is the message we are sending?

Other forms of communication involve body language. This more physical form of connection replicates the canine system (see complete list, above). A leash, be it loose or tight, physically connects us to a dog. A loose leash indicates your green-ring energy, while a taut leash reveals nervousness. Hand signals or whistle sounds for various commands will augment your connection with your dog from various distances. The lowest form of communication with dogs is through words. This may be our No. 1 form of communicating, but words are only minimally useful when communicating with our canine companions. For maximum effect, use words quietly and as little as possible, only one or two words at a time.

# Chapter 20

## Separation Anxiety

*Only the alpha leaves home alone.*

It was a seasonably cold, damp November morning when I met Mary and her dog, Stein. I was chilled to the core. The dog park was unusually quiet, and the dark skies threatened rain or maybe even snow. Satchmo was off wandering around, moving to stay warm. I'd finished raking up the last of the season's leaves and thought about packing up my tools a little early.

As I stood shivering, Mary approached me along with Stein, a Manchester Terrier, and got straight to the point. Separation anxiety.

I asked her to describe Stein's behavior. She said that whenever she and her husband, Philip, left the house they would hear Stein barking and whining at the top of his voice. At this point they were ridden with guilt. Their poor baby was all alone and 'in jail' to-boot, in their very small laundry room. On multiple occasions the neighbours had complained about the disturbing racket coming from their house for hours on end. They had also expressed their concern for Stein's well-being. Typically, Stein was at home alone for about nine hours most days as both Mary and Philip went out to work. From what Mary told me, she and her husband were not the most popular in their neighbourhood.

I asked Mary if Stein did any chewing or damage when alone. "Big time", was her answer. She told me he would chew anything and everything, including the dry wall. He'd ruined the laundry room door.

"The only thing that he hasn't wrecked is the washer and dryer. Sometimes when we get home, Stein is bleeding from the mouth because of his chewing, and often his paws are raw from scratching. The angst that he is experiencing is heart-wrenching."

Their vet had suggested some antidepressants for Stein, and Mary and Philip reluctantly gave it a try. The results were negligible, so they stopped giving them to him. She told me that she and Philip were considering getting rid of Stein because his behavior was also causing problems between the two of them. The guilt and tension they were feeling was coming to a head as they constantly argued about him. They were even considering a trial separation. She felt that her marriage was more important than a dog. However, she couldn't fathom the thought of giving up Stein, their 'only-child'.

At this point I remember hoping that it didn't rain, because I realized how important our conversation had just become. I knew that I was there for a purpose. As we sat on the park bench, I could feel Mary's pain. Her demeanour and tears were pulling on my emotions. I needed to change the negative tone of the discussion.

"Mary, this is totally curable." As soon as I said this, I felt her energy change. Suddenly she felt hope. Boy, those five simple words had a huge effect.

I explained that separation anxiety, for a dog, is the same as for a human. Consider the feeling that a mother would have if she lost her child at the mall, even if the child was only hiding under the coat rack watching her mother have a panic attack. The mother's feelings would be overwhelming, within a few minutes. Think of the anxiety and emptiness after twenty minutes. There are no words to eloquently express that stress.

I asked Mary if Stein had ever been lost. She told me about the time they had been visiting Philip's brother's cottage in Victoria Harbor. Everyone had been sitting outside at the water's edge when they suddenly realized that Stein was missing. Instantly there were four adults and a couple of teenagers on the hunt for their special four-legged friend. After about ten minutes of searching and calling out for Stein, Mary and Philip were beginning to feel sick to their stomachs with panic.

After about thirty minutes, the phone rang. It was Agnes, the owner of the local store down the road. She had discovered Stein at her door, trying to get inside. She recognized him from the day before, when they'd dropped in for ice-cream cones and bought an extra strawberry cone for Stein. Knowing who he belonged to, Agnes phoned Philip's brother. All was good, and instantly Mary and Philip's anxiety dissipated.

I suggested that Stein experienced similar feelings of anxiety when she and Philip left him home alone.

It helps to think like a hard-core canine. The pack leader is the only member to leave the pack on his own. It is the canine law of nature for the leader to leave his pack to check out his territory; to see if other wolves have been marking in the area; to find a water source or accommodation. When a canine leader leaves the pack, the followers accept this without issue. However, if a follower leaves, the alpha experiences anxiety similar to humans', because he can't protect or look after that pack mate. He barks and howls to attract the follower to return to the pack. The desperation and worry are devastating.

I asked Mary, “Does this make sense to you, if you think about things from Stein’s point of view?”

She smiled slightly and slowly nodded. She pondered for a few seconds as she gathered her thoughts and then asked, “Does that mean Stein thinks that he is our leader?”

“Exactly”, I answered. I knew that I could not change Stein’s pack posturing from where we were sitting, so I decided to give Mary some pointers on how to help him with being left alone.

The best route to success is to slowly build on positive behavior with dogs. I suggested that she and Philip start by putting Stein in the laundry room frequently while they were home. The weekend would be an ideal time, as they would have more time to practice. They would not be in a hurry to run off to work and would be in a much calmer state themselves.

“Start by sitting on the floor inside the laundry room. Have Stein come to you and reward and play with him. Give lots of praise and use treats to accelerate the process. The mandate is for him to be comfortable and calm in the laundry room. Both you and Philip should practice this process many times throughout the day, so that he learns to associate the laundry room with fun and rewards.”

“Next, make him stay in the laundry room with the door open. Stand or sit in the doorway so that he cannot leave. After a short period of time, praise and/or treat him. Then let him out and a few minutes later call him back in. Make him stay for a few minutes longer this time. Keep repeating this process until it becomes boring for him, or he begins to get fat from so many treats."

"The next step is to close the laundry-room door with him inside. Only close the door for a few seconds before opening it and praising/treating him for being alone and calm in the room. If he whines or barks, immediately open the door, clap your hands to interrupt his negative behavior and close the door for only about ten seconds. Open the door and praise his calm, quiet behavior, accentuating the positive. Repeat this until you can build up the time so that he remains quiet and calm for about ten minutes. During this process he will know that you are standing outside the door, which will help him through the learning curve."

"Next, build up the length of time and leave him for about 30 minutes while you are home. He will hear you and Philip talking to each other and walking around. Once he remains calm for this length of time, go outside for a short period of time and then come back and praise his calm, quiet behavior. If he starts to bark or whine when you leave or come back inside, open the laundry room door, make some noise; clap, say, "Hey", which will interrupt his whining."

"Next, turn around and walk outside again for about 10 seconds. Return and praise his calm, quiet behavior. He is likely to still be stunned by your previous loud entrance but reward him for being calm and quiet. When you build up the time that you can go outside to about fifteen minutes, your mission will be pretty much accomplished."

"Keep building up the time that you are outside. This whole process should only take a few days if you consciously work at it. You may even want to take a little vacation or time off work to facilitate his continued progress."

"I was thinking the same thing", Mary said.

I suggested to Mary that they have someone let Stein out at midday, especially at first. This would make things easier on him. "As he ages, his bladder won't last the whole day – neither does mine." I also suggested that she and Philip get up about a half-hour earlier in the morning to take Stein for a walk. This would tire him out and help him to relax and sleep while they were away.

Mary's renewed enthusiasm and look of empowerment was gratifying. She gave me a quick kiss on the cheek. I smiled as she headed off to her car with a new zip in her step. Suddenly, Mary stopped in her tracks, turned around and asked if I would be at the park next Sunday. She wanted Philip to meet me. I nodded that I would be here.

As I gathered up my tools, I noticed that I was whistling and realized how great I was feeling. The inclement weather didn't seem so horrible. I could only imagine how great Mary was feeling as she realized that not only could her dog be helped, but also that her marriage was no longer in jeopardy. I was already looking forward to meeting Philip next Sunday.

I whistled for Satchmo as I locked the shed.

**Dog Whisperer Story; a howling Beagle's separation anxiety**

I once received an emergency call from Jake, a young man from a small town about 30 minutes away, regarding his dog's separation anxiety. Several months earlier he moved into a condo complex with his beloved Beagle, Lily. Previously they'd lived with Jake's parents on the family farm, where Lily was rarely alone. The family's Hound was also home, and together they provided companionship for each other.

At the time of his call, Jake was not working and was home most of the time. Whenever he left Lily by herself, she would bark and howl. After many complaints from other tenants in his building, Jake received two separate written notices from the condo management. The second one warned him: "Three times and you're out."

I got Jake's call on a Thursday. He also mentioned that on the following Tuesday he was starting a new job and would need to leave Lily at home, by herself, for eight or nine hours every day.

"Is there any chance that I won't be evicted and have to move back in with my parents?"

I was, of course, encouraging but offered no guarantees.

I arrived at Jake's condo Friday morning and was greeted by a very vocal Beagle as I knocked on the door. Lily seemed to be nervous but friendly. As soon as I put a leash on her, she went quiet and calm. She was quite relaxed and sat beside me as I gave her some friendly rubs. Jake told me that she never settled that way with visitors. I told him that Miss Lily knew that I was not a typical visitor.

Lily had become balanced. It was evident just how natural and comfortable this was for her. After I taught Jake the rules to the Game of Canine, we decided to put Lily to a test by leaving the condo without her. We stood outside the condo door, and Lily whimpered for only a few seconds. After a couple of quiet minutes, we returned, praised Lily to the nth degree and left her again for about ten minutes. There was no sound from Lily as we patiently waited around the corner and down at the far end of the hall, so that she wouldn't hear us. Lily seemed content to have Jake and me leave for this length of time.

I suggested that Jake exercise Lily every morning before leaving for work. He told me that he was a runner and would include Lily on his morning runs. This would help take the edge off Lily's energy level. Jake worked all weekend practicing the rules to the Game of Canine and becoming Lily's new alpha/leader, along with frequently leaving and returning to the condo, so that Lily became complacent about the whole process. In the canine world, it is innate for a pack member to lie-in-wait for the leader to return. Jake reported to me that Lily was an angel from that point forward. On Tuesday, and every day afterwards, Lily was content to calmly and quietly stay home by herself.

The key to keeping Lily in her new pack position was for Jake to live in a black or white world and stringently follow The Recipe.

## Summary

In the canine world it is natural for the leader to leave the pack on his own, but totally unnatural for a follower to leave. By bringing balance to your pack, a dog can overcome separation anxiety very quickly by changing roles from leader to follower. The best analogy is what happens when a parent temporarily loses a child. The anxiety is horrible until the child is located, then it instantly evaporates.

Separation anxiety can also be overcome by approaching the process one small step at a time. Start by leaving your dog alone for only seconds and consistently increase the time alone while praising and rewarding quiet, calm behavior. If your dog shows anxiety then interrupt her, as this is considered negative behavior. Interrupt negative and praise positive behavior.

Humans typically want immediate results. But dog-time is slower than human-time. Imagine that you are on vacation-time and slow down. Dogs cannot skip steps, so please be patient. Keep calm yourself or your dog's behavior will slide backwards. Only a calm owner can have a calm dog.

## Chapter 21

## Control the Door

*A couple of warning barks are ideal.*

Two teenagers were at the dog park one day with their infectiously cute, brilliantly white Bichon Frise, named Max. I noticed that Max was quite submissive to other dogs. If a dog approached, he would instantly roll onto his back with his tail tucked under his belly and pee. This is the canine way of showing total surrender.

The teens, sisters Jacquie and Katie, wandered into the corner where I was fixing a broken fence. Both were soft-spoken and very well mannered. Max was full of spunk and ran up to me. I bent down to give him some rubs. I remembered that I had a dog treat in my pocket and asked Jacquie and Katie if it was OK to give it to Max. They were fine with it. I then asked if he could do any tricks to earn his treat. The girls laughed and told me that he was a total trickster. So I gave the treat to them and asked for a demo. It was too bad I didn't have a bag of treats with me because Max knew a bag of tricks. He was very entertaining and full of personality.

As we chatted, Jacquie and Katie revealed that Max had some serious issues when visitors appeared at their front door. I asked the girls to walk me through an example of what took place.

"Whenever the doorbell rings", Katie said, "Max goes berserk. Intense barking and screaming. A very high-pitched squeal like he is being killed as he pounces on the door."

"It's a good thing the door opens inward and not outward", said Jacquie, "because otherwise he would break the latch."

"Wow", I said. "Is he aggressive with visitors?"

"Not in the least", Jacquie said. "He's the friendliest dog that you could possibly have. He is just off the wall with excitement when people visit. He jumps about four feet off the ground, trying to lick their faces. I'm afraid it's offensive to some."

I asked how they handled all this insanity when the doorbell rings. They told me they'd usually just yell and scream at him from various parts of the house. If someone was home alone with him and they were busy, say on the phone or in the shower, they had to stop whatever they were doing, or Max would scratch the door and carry on until they forced him to stop.

I then asked how they stopped him. They said that they picked him up and gave him a treat, so that he would go quiet. This allowed them to open the door in peace.

I quickly explained the concept of the Game of Canine. I then asked, "Who is scoring all the points?"

"Certainly not us", Katie laughed.

"The good news", I said, "is that Max is extremely smart. I've seen his trick repertoire. The bad news is that he is a spoiled brat, who gets exactly what he wants."

They both smiled and nodded. "That's our Max", said Jacquie.

I mentioned that it is very easy to treat our dogs like humans. "For example, if a young child is with you while you're answering the door, it would be logical to pick up the child so that you have total control of her and at the same time she would feel safe and protected. She cannot run out the door or get under foot while you're welcoming visitors. If you pick up an excited dog, however, it's a form of praise. Think about it. Your dog is grossly misbehaving by barking, jumping, screaming and pounding the door as he has a tantrum. Then you pick him up and lay some love on him.

From his point of view, he is expecting you to praise him because you pick him up every time someone visits. No wonder he keeps it up with such intensity. Not only does he get picked up and loved, but he gets a treat as well. When he does one of his tricks, he is rewarded with a treat. It's no different, from his point of view." He says, 'I perform, and you guys love me and treat me. Do you want me to bark louder or scream more? Keep treating me and I'll keep up the shenanigans.'

At this point both Jacquie and Katie had a light-bulb moment. Without belabouring the point, I told them that I wanted to introduce them to an important rule in the Game of Canine. The rule is: *I control the door, from afar and near* (see rule No. 4 in Chapter 29; "Six Ways to Say, I'm the Leader, Not You"). This is a rule that their whole household needs to master. My guess is Max will learn this rule in very short order.

(In the wild canine world, there is always a sentry to keep watch. If the sentry senses danger, he quietly alerts the alpha, who makes an executive decision to freeze, fight or run. If the sentry started barking profusely, this would notify their adversary of their location. But this would never happen, as their warning system is virtually silent.)

**Control the door from afar**

Next, I said to them, "If you are expecting a visitor, I suggest that you put a leash on Max beforehand. It won't matter where you are in the house. He will be at your side, with the leash in hand. As soon as the doorbell rings and he launches into his usual frenzy, your job is to quickly calm him."

"A fundamental in the Game of Canine is: *Control the calm to win the game*", I said. "If you can calm him within five seconds, then you score a point in the Game of Canine. If his excitement continues for more than five seconds, it will be Max who scores. If he continues to wreak havoc, he scores a point every five seconds thereafter. Every point you score in the Game of Canine is at the expense of your opponent. If you score he gives up a point, and when Max scores it is you who forfeits a point. It's like volleyball where a point is scored on every play." Jacquie and Katie understood.

"In order to get Max calm", I said, "stand in front of him, facing him, while you stand between him and the door. Don't yell at him. In fact, don't talk to him at all. Your objective is to interrupt him and have him refocus on you. Sharply say, 'Hey', as you give the leash a quick flick or pop. You could also clap your hands to interrupt him. Stand tall and don't bend over. Use your height as a posture of strength. Keep calm and wait him out. After he's remained calm for about ten seconds, as his short-term memory fills with only calm energy, praise and treat him. This will encourage repetition of the calm process. Always praise and/or treat the positive only.

Next, proceed in the direction of the door. If he starts to ramp up his excitement again, stop and calm him once again. Continue controlling the calm until you get to about eight feet from the door. The next step is to give him a sit/stay command. This will become his special place to always wait when visitors arrive. You are now in total control and ready to answer the door with a calm dog waiting in a sit/stay position." I told the girls that I would describe how to answer the door in a minute. (see Chapter 26; "Six Ways to Interrupt Negative Behavior" for a complete list of interruption techniques).

**Control the door from near**

When someone unexpectedly rings the doorbell, Max's reaction is to bark incessantly as he runs to the door and pounces on it.

"Your job, girls, is to quickly and quietly approach him", I said. "There should be no yelling at him from other rooms; we know how ineffective that is. As you reach him, step in front of him, with your back to the door and say, 'Hey'. Clap your hands as you step into his space/face. The whole idea is for you, the leaders of the pack, to take control of the door area. By interrupting his negative behavior and creating a calm, you'll score a point in the Game of Canine.

Next, shoo him back about eight feet from the door and slip a leash on him. Once again, this position will become his special place whenever there are visitors. Just as when you controlled the door from afar and brought him to his special place, he should now be sitting calmly, waiting for further direction from you, and not fixated on the door.

What takes place next will be reflective of the level of his obedience training. Give him the command to sit/stay. Take your time. Dog-time is slower than human time. I suggest that you practice this with family members who can go outside and ring the doorbell to create the scenario that you must overcome. Also, you must implement the Golden Rule; *Tell him once and never take no for an answer.* He must obey the order given by you (see Chapter 29; "Six Ways to Interrupt Negative Behavior"). At this point it is imperative that he calmly remains in a sit/stay position.

"In the early stages of practicing this behavior, even if you don't get to answer the door, consider it a victory and give yourself some points, as you control the calm. Your family member may even walk away after ringing the bell the first few times you practice. When all is quiet outside, Max won't have a need to focus on the door. Keep practicing with faux visitors until you have total calm control over Max. This will exponentially improve the results with legitimate visitors."

"At this point, you and your dog will have mastered *from afar and from near*. You'll be able to position Mr. Max in his special place whenever visitors arrive. Keep a leash on him to maintain total control. This specific spot should always be maintained."

"The next step is to answer the door while preserving a calm from Max. My favorite question, which can be asked in every situation is, *when did I give up control?* The answer needs to be, *I did not give up control.*"

"At this point, if you were to turn your back on him to answer the door, you would most certainly be giving up control, and he would very likely bolt to the door. If you take your eyes off your dog, in any circumstance, the level of your control is diluted as per the length of time that you are not watching him, so it's necessary to keep your eyes on Max, even if it is from a peripheral view.

I told them, "The only way to keep your eye on him and answer the door at the same time is to turn sideways to both Max and the door, so that you can very quickly turn your head back and forth. Your main subject is Max; therefore, I suggest that you never take your focus or eyes off him for more than a split second to glance at your guests. By maintaining a sideway stance, he remains in your peripheral view, just as your visitor does. You can easily talk to them while looking in Max's direction. If he starts to move or get excited, you will be able to immediately catch him with an interrupting 'Hey' sound as you step back into his space/face and reset him in his sit/stay position." Simply say to your guest, "Max is in training". This is the most impactful statement one can say when other people are involved with you and your dog.

I find that people are extremely respectful whenever I say this to them. It seems to stimulate compassion, because it has such a positive connotation to it.

"Have your guest step into the house, as you keep your focus on Max", I said. "Also ask them to totally ignore Max: no eye contact, talking to him or any other connection. As you continue to maintain a calm, don't praise him too early, as the exercise is not complete until you are ready to leave the door area and proceed to another room. If the visitor wants to engage with him and Max is controlling himself, even if he is wiggling his rump and tail, then his reward will be to be released from his sit/stay position and meet-and-greet your guest. If, however, you want to keep Max from meeting the person (say they are afraid of dogs, they don't want him to jump on their good clothes or they are a delivery person), then he must remain in his sit/stay position until you decide to release him."

"Practice makes perfect", I said to Jacquie and Katie. "If you want to get good at shooting three-point baskets, you must practice shooting the ball."

"We understand", said Jacquie. Continuing, I said, "Whenever a family member arrives home, he or she should call from their car to give a heads-up and then ring the doorbell and wait until someone answers the door. Whoever is home with Max can leash him and practice the new process of answering the door. If more than one person is at home, keep rotating who has control of the leash, so everyone gets to master this process."

Katie asked, "Is this the same process that we use to control him if we're at the park and he wants to jump on kids or if we're walking down the street and he wants to accost everyone we come across?"

"Absolutely", I said. "You must *control the calm to win the game,* anytime, anywhere and in any situation." I suggested that they *imagine* what it would be like to have control of Max in all circumstances. "While walking down the street or at the park, *imagine* him obeying the sit/stay command and waiting calmly for your next command. With the end in your mind, knowing your expectations, it is your job to demand that Max gives you these results. Mr. Smarty Pants is most certainly capable of learning this level of obedience, as all dogs are."

The alpha leader of a pack of wild canines can instantly calm his pack. Consider a situation when the alpha senses danger and he needs his pack to become quiet and calm within a split second to avoid notifying the intruder of their whereabouts. A canine can go calm in the snap of a finger. If Max perceives Jacquie and Katie, as well as other family members, to be leaders/alphas, he will readily give them a calm when commanded to do so. It is a must, for all family members, to position themselves, from Max's perspective, very high on their own Leader Ladders.

To help with pack posturing in their home, I suggested that Jacquie and Katie put a leash on Max, about seventy-five percent of the time, for about a week. This will mean that whenever someone is home and not sleeping, he will be attached to someone most of the time. From the canine end of the leash, it means that the dog must keep track of the humans. If the human gets up to move around the home, then Max must react and keep up with them. This makes him subservient and you superior in the pecking order.

I can't stress how effective in pack realignment this exercise is.

**Dog Whisperer Story; the behemoth Malamute**

I was called to a home where a 120-pound Alaskan Malamute was causing huge problems whenever visitors arrived at the front door. First, Radar would bellow a loud, deep bark for all to hear. When visitors entered, he would jump and try to lick them, often knocking them over. All this was done in a friendly way with absolutely no intent of aggression. He was simply demanding that guests play with him. From Radar's point of view, he was saying, "Pay homage to me. I want attention. I'm important. I'm in charge around here." This was, however, very stressful for owners Richard and Talia, along with their two teenagers, Lauren and Spike, because they had no control whatsoever.

As soon as I rang the doorbell, Radar went off like a bomb, causing instant chaos. Not only was there a dog with a huge, deep voice barking loudly, there were also several humans screaming at him. I heard at least three people yell out his name, accompanied by, "Shut-up, quiet, come and stop it", along with some other things that I can't repeat.

The question was, "Who is scoring points in the Game of Canine?" I'd say the score was at least 10-0 for Radar. I figured that I was in for a tough night, with an out-of-control dog, compounded by out-of-control humans.

As the door opened, good-old-boy Radar predictably just wanted my attention. Due to his enormity, any negative behavior could make for an unpleasant visitor experience. If someone was the least bit wary of dogs, this was not the door to knock on. As he got close to me, I immediately put a slip-lead on him and stepped forward into his space, with my thighs touching his snout. I gave the leash a quick light pop and sharply said, "Hey". Next, I put my hands above his head, like an evangelist healer, and gave him a calm, strong stare. He stopped all previous exuberance and immediately settled in a sit position.

The four human members of the pack were dumbfounded. All of them had their mouths wide open as they asked me what kind of magic that was? I jokingly answered that I had magic fairy dust in my pockets and once Radar got a whiff of it, he was all mine. They all laughed. I then gave Radar a rub to praise his calm behavior.

I proceeded to explain, "You cannot have a calm dog if you are not calm yourself. Calm, strong, leader-energy is exactly what Radar needs and wants." At that point, if Radar could have talked he would have said, "Bruce, save me from this chaotic, unstable environment. There is no leadership here. Welcome, great leader. How can I serve you?"

Radar didn't take his eyes off me for the whole visit, and he behaved like a saint for the duration. He enjoyed the new pack balance implicitly. He never stopped smiling.

Dogs cannot respect or follow inconsistency or instability. Remember that energy is the No. 1 way to communicate in the canine language. From their viewpoint, we owners are either doing things the canine way or we are not. It's a treat for me when I get to work with both smart people and smart dogs, as was the case with Richard and his family. They were all extremely receptive to my lessons. They agreed to go a week without saying a word to Mr. Radar, and focus on communicating with him using energy, body language, a loose leash and hand signals. This would eliminate all yelling and screaming. I bet the neighbours enjoyed the peace and quiet.

On my second visit, I thought that no one was home when I arrived because of the absence of chaos when I rang the doorbell. Radar was about five percent as vocal as he'd been on the previous visit. This was a radical improvement. It was another victory for humans learning the Game of Canine. Before, Richard had been the most vocal with Radar. I asked them how they did without talking to him. "We made a big joke out of it whenever someone got caught breaking the rules", Talia said. "All we had to ask is – Are you following The Recipe?" They all looked at one another and laughed.

When a dog barks at someone at the door or something outside the home and his barks are short and incessant, this cadence of bark indicates his nervous insecurity. It's as if he is saying, "My pack is here. Stay away, I'm warning you." He feels obligated to go into the protective mode. This kind of bark can be classified as insecure/dominant behavior, which can result in fear aggression. If he barks only once or twice, possibly accompanied with a deep, long growl, he is likely warning the humans inside the house as well as anyone on the outside. This is balanced, confident, follower behavior.

**Summary**

Yelling and screaming are totally ineffective forms of communication with canines. They create exactly what you don't want; instability, resulting in ranking confusion and disrespect within the pack. It also forces your dog to take on the alpha role due to the leadership void created by the humans.

When your dog won't listen to you, think about how you are conveying your message. If a small dog is picked up whenever she misbehaves, she will perceive this as praise, love and reward. This only encourages the negative behavior to be repeated. When your dog is barking and carrying on while someone is at the door, it is imperative to calm her. By calmly interrupting and getting into a dog's face/space, you are taking control of the situation and showing leadership. Therefore, your dog will be forced to assume the follower role. Once she is calm and then you pick her up, you would be praising calm behavior. In a combo-pack, it is the human leader's job to: *Control the door, from afar and near.* The mission is to maintain a calm dog throughout the whole process.

Don't forget to praise/treat your dog for obeying any command. This will encourage her to repeat the positive behavior. You need to let her know what pleases you. There can never be too much positive praise or too many rewards unless, of course, your dog is packing on some extra pounds from too many treats. If so, try giving her something more nutritious, such as carrots or celery. They are, crunchy, moist, flavorsome and good for her.

# Chapter 22

## Human Aggression

*Aggression comes in multiple levels.*

One Sunday morning my work at the park was at a standstill while I thought about a talk I was giving the following day. Suddenly my thoughts were interrupted by the sounds of screaming, yelling, snarling and barking. In a flash I automatically swung around and started to move toward the hub of activity. Satchmo caught up to me and stopped me in my tracks. I gave him a quick hand signal along with a firm voice command to 'stay'. Another dog in the mix would only exacerbate the chaos.

A Golden Retriever was in a rage, his aggression focused on a lady holding her tiny terrified Italian Grayhound puppy. I ran toward them at full speed, with thoughts about how I could defuse the situation, along with my own safety in the forefront of my mind. It was a bit of a hike halfway across the park near the front gate. The man who owned the Golden Retriever was desperately trying to put a leash on him and get control of the situation. He was doing a poor job at best. His dog was massive in stature and was raging, snarling and barking at the woman and her panic-stricken puppy.

As I approached, good luck struck, the man finally got his dog leashed. The Golden Retriever's behavior was now somewhat under control, albeit he was still barking and growling. Immediately the lady started to yell and scream, as if it was her turn to let loose with a barrage of aggressive expletives aimed at the man. I'm sure that she felt justified.

I was oblivious to what had transpired in the first place, but I was about to get the whole picture. As I caught my breath, after my morning sprint, the story soon became clear. When the Golden Retriever first approached the tiny Italian Greyhound puppy, the lady had been uncomfortable with her dog being in what she perceived to be a precarious position, possibly dangerous. She panicked and started yelling at the Golden Retriever to get away from her dog. I say panicked because the puppy was apparently at no risk whatsoever. As his owner later explained, the Golden Retriever was extremely friendly to dogs, just not people-friendly. The lady had placed herself in the Golden Retriever's space and he'd reacted by snarling, growling and snapping at her.

I can't totally blame the Golden Retriever. After all, she ran into his space, yelling and waving her hands in a threatening manner. His owner kept saying that his dog hadn't been causing any problems and that the lady had created the whole mess.

She walked away with her pup tucked under her arm, yelling that his dog should be put down because of his aggression. The good news is that no one, dog or human, was hurt in the ruckus. But the owners were shocked, fearful, angry and upset.

I had a chance to chat with the Golden Retriever's owner after the indignant and rather expressive lady had made her way through the park gate. His name was Alan, and his dog was Sidney. Alan's wife, Wendy, soon showed up. She'd been watching the whole scene from their car, where she'd been resting due to muscle spasms in her lower back, which made walking very uncomfortable.

They started telling me about how wonderful Sidney was, except for his people-aggression. He had only bitten one person, the pizza delivery guy, a couple of days ago. Wendy expressed her embarrassment over what just happened and wondered if they should consider asking their vet about medicating Sidney. She and Alan talked about their growing concern about Sidney's increasing level of aggression.

With a look of despair, they mentioned the possibility of euthanasia. Alan said, "Sid is almost two years old and things have been seriously getting worse in the aggression department over the last few months. The pizza-guy incident happened when I was standing in the front hallway, and Sid was sitting quietly beside me, intently focused on the delivery guy. When he put his hand out to take the money, Sid lunged at him and bit his arm. Luckily the coat the guy was wearing protected him enough so that the skin was not broken."

Alan and Wendy had been mortified by this event.

"I hope you gave the guy a big tip", I said. "*Extra* generous", Wendy said. They were also pleasantly surprised that they didn't hear from the pizza company about the incident.

"Why did he react with a bite?" Wendy asked. "Why did he feel that he had to protect Alan when the truth of the matter is that he didn't have to protect either us at all? There was absolutely no threat whatsoever."

My guess was that there was a melding of several factors, including Sid's continuous progression of dominance, the delivery man's fear, and Alan's nervous concern. These factors were enough to tip the balance. Alan and Wendy said that up to that weekend Sid had only barked at people: no lunging or snapping. With the pizza guy, and today at the park, were the only times that he had been so forward with his aggression.

I asked about Sid's barking at people from inside the house or when he was in the backyard. The answer was that Sid barked in both cases. Alan said, "It seems that he is on-guard when in the house or yard. He sits on the couch in the front window, staring endlessly outside, keeping a vigilant watch. From the yard he can see the street through the gate at the side of the house. In both places he barks whenever someone passes by. He doesn't seem to bother with other dogs, cats or squirrels. Obviously, Sid has a singular focus of aggression towards humans."

I suggested that today had been a reactive situation, as the lady got into his space while yelling and waving her arms. Sid's behavior, of course, had been unbecoming, and a plan had to be put in place to eliminate any further acts of aggression. I introduced them to a few basic rules to the Game of Canine. I also mentioned that dominance and aggression are both progressive behavioral traits that they had been experiencing. If his aggression continued to increase, the result could be devastating for Sid, Alan, Wendy or anyone else on the receiving end of Sid's pearly white canines. And it could ultimately put Sid's life at risk because Alan and Wendy would likely feel the need to put him down.

Consistent, strong human leadership will cure canine misbehaviors, prevent future problems as well as build trust and respect. To eradicate aggressive incidents with Sid, Alan and Wendy had to learn to become masters at the Game of Canine. I introduced the concept of my favorite question; *When did I give up control?* To maintain control, I suggested that they keep Sid close to them by leashing him always when other people are nearby, whether indoors or out, and to focus on a calm, strong leader-energy while working with him. I also mentioned to be aware of the leash: loose versus tight. A tight leash gives off tension, while a loose leash represents green-ring leader-energy. The key for them was to focus on insightful management.

"You must be on top of every situation before it takes place", I told them. "If you are not proactive, Sid's behavior could be dangerous. If you use forethought, you will be far more successful at controlling the game."

*Control the calm to win the game.*

I knew that this would be easy for them to do, as they were seriously motivated to eliminate any future problems. I also suggested they put something in front of the window in their living room to prevent Sid from assuming his usual position of being on guard-duty. If he could not see out the window, he would be able to relax and enjoy an off-duty role. Wendy mentioned that they had previously talked about rearranging the living room furniture, so this was an ideal time for them to do so.

I asked about their backyard set up. Would they be able to block the view of the street through the gate? They thought a temporary solution would be to tack up an old 'For Sale' sign that they had in the garage. I mentioned that if Sid started barking at people walking past the house, they needed to interrupt him immediately and make him leave the location. The best plan would be for them to join him whenever he was in the yard. By keeping Sid in check at his two favorite places to bark, the front window and yard, they would be well on their way to relegating him to the position of follower. I added that I would look forward to seeing them at the park in the coming weeks for updates on their progress, and to call me if they had any questions.

**Dog Whisperer Story; the angry St. Bernard**

I was contacted by a dog owner whose panic and desperation were immediately evident in her voice. Her enormous four-year-old 200-pound St. Bernard, named Griffin, had bitten her best friend in the face. The very thought was horrific. I winced when she told me.

Nancy went on to tell me about all the people who wanted to put Griffin down. I immediately wondered if her friend was at the top of the list. Apparently, she was not even on the list because she had known and loved Griff all his life. Nancy's vet had told her that he must be put down, as he could never be trusted again and would likely repeat his behavior. The local animal shelter somehow got wind of the bite and reiterated the same belief. Lastly was the city health official who insisted that the dog be quarantined for ten days, the time it would take to officially establish whether the dog had rabies. After the quarantine period he recommended to Nancy that he be put to sleep. Nancy was beside herself. She didn't know what to do. Her best friend had a face full of stitches, but Nancy loved her dog like any other family member. It was the first time Griffin had bitten anyone.

Nancy also had a young eight-month-old St. Bernard named Beau. All in all, Beau was extremely friendly to everyone, but was starting to mimic Griffin's aggressive behavior whenever the doorbell rang; a classic copy-cat syndrome.

Nancy asked me what I thought. Did I think that Griffin could be saved even though everyone wanted him destroyed? I asked if she would give me five minutes with Griffin. She wondered what could possibly be accomplished in five minutes. I told her I would then know if Griffin could be balanced or not. I added that I had yet to meet a dog that could not be balanced, because realignment of pack ranking is a natural law of canine nature.

"I have called several trainers and not one seemed to think there was any chance of saving him", she said. "I called a different vet from my own for a second opinion. She suggested that I call you because of the great results you had with some of her clients' dogs who exhibited extreme aggression."

We set up a time for me to come to her home. She and her husband Vern lived in a small town about an hour and a half away from me. I asked her to send me photos of Big Griff, as she called him, and told her that I needed a measurement of his snout, because I would be using a muzzle with him.

I like to use a cage style of muzzle, which covers the dog's whole snout versus one that slides over his snout and is tightened so that he cannot open his mouth. The problems with this second style of muzzle are twofold: (1) The dog is automatically put into a negative frame of mind because his mouth is clamped closed and he can't even pant properly; (2) He can still bite using his incisors, or front teeth.

A cage muzzle goes over his whole snout, encompassing his nose and front teeth. He can pant, drink or even chew a treat, should you slip something through the slots. What it doesn't do is put the dog in a negative frame of mind, so there is one less obstacle to overcome.

Obviously, a huge dog like Big Griff required a huge muzzle. I had to special-order one to accommodate such a large boy. He was the size of a small bear . . . an angry bear. Upon my arrival I asked Nancy, Vern and their adult son Mark to come outside while I explained the muzzle and leash system that I wanted them to use. While we were outside talking, I could hear both dogs aggressively barking and carrying on inside the front hallway of their home. Two giant aggressive dogs produce a lot of commotion. Part of my instruction was to keep Beau in another room. I didn't need the double whammy of dealing with two dogs at the same time, especially when Griffin alone would be a physical, as well as mental, handful. Physically, he weighed about as much as me.

Before I entered the house, I calmed myself by taking several deep breaths and focusing on my energy. I knew this would be a key strength in the process because Griffin would sense my energy. If I entered and said to myself, "Wow, you didn't tell me he was *that* bad. What the heck am I doing here?" this would trigger Griffin's predator instinct and encourage him to attack me. On the other hand, if I said to myself, "I thought you were supposed to be bad. You're not so tough. I'm not afraid of you", he would sense my calm, strong, green-ring energy. He would know that I wasn't afraid and was not giving off any aggression signals.

As I walked into the house, Nancy was following my instructions. She kept Griffin a safe distance back from the door, muzzled and leashed with the slip lead that I gave her, and kept herself between him and the front door. This allowed him to sense me and feel me out, even though he was aggressive and giving Nancy a hard time as he tried to get to me. In these situations, I didn't initially make eye contact with him because it would be perceived as a challenge. I waited for a few seconds to allow him to sense my energy.

Next, I told Nancy to hand me the leash as I made strong eye contact with him. Griff and I got into a bit of a pushing match for a short period of time. I had the advantage of him being leashed and muzzled (for my safety). He was snarling, with his lips curled up and showing me all his teeth and gums. He was trying to control the situation and 'eat me'. However, he became calm and respectful much quicker than I expected, which was a big bonus for me. He sat and looked up at me as if to say, "What's next boss?"

At this time, I asked that Beau be brought to me. I knew that at his young age he would not be an issue. He immediately went into a respectful, follower mode. After all, his big brother was already exhibiting this mindset and behavior, so he readily followed suit.

The family and I sat at the dining room table for the next couple of hours as I taught them the Game of Canine. Both Big Griff and Beau were perfect gentlemen throughout this process. They also remained calm and respectful when we walked outside. A neighbour happened to be out at the same time and was impressed by how well behaved both dogs were. She, of course, had witnessed the old Griff and Beau when they were at their aggressive worst. Both dogs walked respectfully beside me, at first, and then Nancy and Vern. Mission accomplished for today.

Upon my return visit there, I did not hear a single bark or sound when I rang the doorbell. I was beginning to wonder if anyone was home when Vern answered the door and asked me to come in. As I was entering I asked him where Nancy and the dogs were, thinking that they must be out for a walk. He told me that they were in the kitchen. I looked over his shoulder to see two calm, well-behaved dogs sitting on either side of Nancy. I was blown away by Nancy's level of achievement in only one week. She had total leadership control over two enormous, *follower,* St. Bernards. She had climbed her Leader Ladder to at least the 90-percent level.

My second session with clients is much shorter in length than the first, because typically there are only minor adjustments to be made. In Nancy and Vern's case, they had such unprecedented success in one week that my presence was almost not required. We chatted for about twenty minutes about how wonderful the dogs were doing, especially Griffin. Nancy and Vern had almost nothing negative to tell me. Big Griff was the happiest he'd been since he was a puppy and gave them all the respect that they could have hoped for. Walking and greeting guests at the door was now a simple matter, and they had total control. Nancy said, "I'm over the moon with your service and teachings, Bruce. The Recipe, or rules to your Game of Canine, are life-altering. I can't wait to take Griff back to my vet, who insisted that I euthanize him. I just want to prove to him how wrong he was."

Of all the clients that I have worked with in my career, Nancy, who is in her 60s, was undoubtedly one of the fastest in climbing to the top of her Leader Ladder. Obviously winning the Game of Canine is not about power, strength or being a tough guy. All one must do is follow The Recipe as stringently as possible.

Back to Nancy's original question: "Did I think that Griffin could be saved even though everyone wanted him put down?" My answer; "Do you have five minutes?"

**The following additional story is about dog aggression to the *maximum* level.**

## I Believe They're All Savable

*Eradicate the confusion to produce good behavior.*

My theory that all dogs are savable, unless there is a medical issue, was challenged to the nth degree when I met Lucien, a rescued Belgian Malinois. His owners, a sister and brother sharing a house while studying to become doctors, couldn't bear the thought of him being put down, even though he had bitten many people as well as themselves on many occasions.

I am frequently asked, "What was the worst dog you have ever encountered?" I have met dogs with extreme behavioral issues in various categories, e.g., nervous insecurity, uncontrollable exuberance and disrespect, as well as aggression toward humans and dogs. I had to create an entirely new category for Lucien; *Ultimate Aggression*. He had a notorious history of attacking both people and dogs.

There are different levels of canine aggression. The worst, or purest form, is when a dog leaves his post, or position, to attack someone. Lucien stretched the measuring stick in this department. The list of his attacks and bites was almost unimaginable. "How many people or dogs has he bitten and drawn blood?" I asked Vivienne and Leo.

"This year?" Vivian said. "Over twenty-five times so far this year. That includes both dogs and humans. The bulk of those bites have been with my family, relatives and friends while in our home. Only a few have been on the street while walking and at the local ball park."

That qualifies as *ultimate aggression.* I was shocked that Lucien was still alive and had not been put down. I guess it was a good thing that most of his bites were with family members, who didn't report him to the police or the city.

Understandably, Lucien was in a precarious position. They had already tried several dog trainers, and I was his last hope; it was me or the needle. I had to teach Viv and Leo the workings of the canine mind to save him. But first I had to balance him.

Upon entering a home, the typical time frame for me to balance a dog is only a few minutes, some a little longer and some in just a few seconds. Lucien broke the mold. He took an hour and fifteen minutes before finally surrendering to me. During these seventy-five minutes he was relentless as he attacked me more than twenty times. It's a good thing he was muzzled. During the process I asked myself several times, "Is this going to be the first dog that I have met that cannot be balanced? Is he so disturbed that he can't surrender to me?" I also knew that if I was unsuccessful he would not live for more than twenty-four hours, so my persistence and determination not to give up on him were essential.

When he was finally exhausted, he surrendered and lay down in the prone position on his side, indicating the deepest level of calm. It was as if Lucien had been reborn.

He wasn't the only one who needed a power nap. Fortunately, I came away unscathed but for a few scratches on my arms from his paws. Throughout the whole process I'd maintained green-ring energy with no fear or aggression. I frequently riled him up, causing him to attack me. I knew he had to release all his aggression and wear out before I had a chance of winning the battle. He was ruthless in his mission to hold onto his alpha status. Afterwards, through their tears, Viv and Leo commented on my impregnable, calm energy and that I didn't give up on him.

When I was a kid my dad used to call me Mr. Persistent. It sure paid off that day.

On my second visit, Lucien barked only once when I rang the doorbell. When I went inside, he was calmly lying down in the kitchen, off-duty. There was no barking or agitation, just a big smile with his tongue hanging out the side of his mouth. I said to them, "Ain't balance beautiful?"

Lucien's story confirms my theory: "They're all Savable."

## Summary

People often feel that a dog should be destroyed because of bad behavior. Bad behavior is a relative term to different people.

When I work with a client whose dog has bitten and injured someone, their vet will often suggest that they euthanize the dog because they have 'crossed the line' and can never go back. I have heard this on far too many occasions. Fortunately, I can say that I have been able to save all the dogs that I have worked with that have 'crossed the so-called line'. The fundamental fix is to first realign the pack pecking order and then consistently follow the rules to the Game of Canine.

One occasion, a client called me almost a year after I worked with her family, to tell me their Cane Corso was biting again, and they were considering putting the dog down. I asked her where they keep the rules. She said, "In my filing cabinet."

"No one is reading them in there", I said.

I suggested that she get out the rules to review with her family while they were having dinner. It would quickly become evident to them that they have slipped back into the gray human zone.

"If all family members go back to playing tightly to the rules (black or white) and your dog doesn't stop biting, I will come to your house immediately", I said. I also told her that I would call in three days to see how they were progressing.

When I phoned she reported that her dog had gone back to his balanced friendly way and she and her family *accepted* responsibility for causing the problem behavior.

This back and forth crossing the line is purely reflective of dog owners crossing the line themselves. When owners stay on the leader's side, their dog will happily remain on the follower's side of the hypothetical line.

## Chapter 23

## Children and Newborn Babies in the Pack

*Pack leaders come in all ages and sizes.*

It was a wonderful sunny May morning at the dog park as the sun's rays filtered through the budding tree branches. The saying, 'spring was in the air' was a welcome thought after a rather long and harsh winter. It was one of those special days that make it difficult to be in a bad mood. Buds were bursting, tulips were poking their heads through last year's leaves, and the air smelled sweet and fresh.

I looked around as I heard someone calling out my name, "Brewster". A young couple was fast approaching in tow behind a couple of large Doodles. I wasn't sure if they were Goldendoodles or Labradoodles, but they sure made a handsome pair. My assumption was that the dogs were siblings because they looked like each other; same size, color and grooming. Each dog was wearing a harness attached to a short nylon leash. Each harness and leash was a matching color; either blue or pink.

As the group progressed up the slope toward me, I turned to Satchmo and gave him a whistle command to 'Stay', even though he was already quietly obeying the same command from about an hour before. I felt that being proactive and repeating myself would ensure that he remained where he was.

The couple seemed to be on a mission to seek me out. And it turned out the mission was serious. The woman was obviously very pregnant. If her due date had been yesterday, I wouldn't have been surprised. They introduced themselves as David and Susan. Their dogs were Digby and Jersey.

I shook the couple's hands but didn't acknowledge either of the dogs, who were excitingly pulling on their leashes, trying to move toward Satchmo. David and Susan were both catching their breath as they tried in vain to get control of their dogs. I consciously ignored the chaos until I could no longer tolerate seeing both dogs controlling the situation and scoring all the points at will. I instinctively reacted with a clap of my hands while simultaneously saying, "Hey", with conviction, and stepping into their space. The dogs diverted their attention from Satchmo as they looked up at me, then went calm and quiet.

"Wow", David said. "No wonder your reputation precedes you. We want some of that. Does it come in a bottle?"

"I wish it did. I'd be dripping in wealth." We all laughed.

I turned to Susan and asked when she was due. "Four weeks", she said, in a curt voice. She was all business as she refocused the discussion on their dogs' problems. "How can we ensure that our baby will be safe with these two crazy, uncontrollable bouncy dogs?"

I thought to myself, "That's a very serious question indeed". I was sensing Digby and Jersey's escalating excitement, so once again I made strong eye contact to message them to remain seated and calm, which they did.

(Humans also stare to communicate. Like most of us, I remember the stare that my mother would give me when I was being bad as a kid. It was razor sharp and was *not* to be challenged. It was

100 percent the opposite to the warm, smiling look of love that I remember her for. I use this staring technique with Satchmo sometimes, when he is being impish. Canine leaders routinely use this very effective form of communication to send a message to a member of their pack.)

I asked David and Susan to give me some examples of when they felt out of control with their dogs.

Susan was pensive: "All the time", she said. "When people come to visit, which isn't very often anymore; when walking down the street as people or dogs walk past; when we come home from work; when we feed them; and just about any other time they decide to act up. David and I have no control over them whatsoever. In fact, I can't think of any time when we have total control."

I was taken aback and a little hesitant to respond. I wasn't sure if I should laugh, because David had a big grin on his face while looking at Susan.

"I can certainly understand your concern about having an infant in the home. The great news is that Digby and Jersey's exuberance can be managed without much effort."

"Obviously you have control", David said. "I can't believe they are calm and respectful of you – and you haven't said anything to them. I am dumbfounded that they haven't molested you and your dog, who, I might add, is impressively well behaved. I would give anything for our dogs to be as obedient as yours. Would you like to move into our house?"

"I am frequently asked to move in with families. I could be a homeless nomad and move from house to house. Satchmo's behavior just goes to show you what Digby and Jersey are capable of. You have a month to overcome this hurdle and create a safe environment for your newborn. I will happily guide you through this process."

"I'm already feeling better. I can't believe these are my dogs", Susan said.

The first thing that I pointed out was the leash system they were using. A harness encourages a dog to pull, and it does not give much control unless the dog is small enough to be lifted off the ground by the harness. Even though a small dog can be physically controlled by a harness, it still promotes pulling because it feels good.

Dogs that need a harness are: a dog leading a blind person; a tracking dog; and a sled dog pulling either a sled or a cart.

I suggested that their dogs needed a correctional collar system such as a slip lead, which would effectively help David and Susan get control. I offered them two that I had in the car, *gratis.* I had used them with Satchmo but didn't need to use them much anymore. I fibbed a little bit. Occasionally I do use a slip lead with Satchmo, mostly to make other people feel comfortable when they don't know him. It is my responsibility and obligation to prevent anyone from feeling nervous or uncomfortable whenever Satchmo is near them.

I suggested that we all walk over to my car, which was much easier said than done. I focused on maintaining Satchmo's calm while these two rambunctious characters were barking, pulling and jumping all over the place. It was anarchy and chaos at the same time. These dogs were on thin ice as David and Susan considered looking for a new home for them before their newborn arrived. We had a super-size job to do, with only a sliver of time.

After I had Satchmo jump into the back of my car, I presented the slip leads to them and showed them how they work. I said, "Slip leads are quite simple and very effective. If your dogs pull, the lead gets tighter. If they relax their pulling, the lead automatically loosens. Also, if you give a gentle correction with a quick, light pop on the lead when they pull, they will be interrupted as their focus is redirected to you."

I put a slip lead on Digby before I removed his harness; I didn't want to give up control and not have at least one leash on him, due to his explosive energy. Then I proceeded to walk him around the parking lot. If he pulled ahead, I gave a light pop and changed direction. After this happened a few times, he kept his focus on me and walked like a champ. I erratically changed my speed between walking slow to running a short distance. Digby obediently walked beside me like a graduate of an obedience class. I repeated the process with Jersey with equal results.

"If we can achieve a fraction of what you just did", Susan said, "I will be ecstatic".

I replied, "It only shows you what they are capable of".

I suggested that she and David give it a try with a dog each. After a few minutes of practice, with lots of encouragement and direction, they accomplished similar results.

The look of revelation on both David and Susan's faces was heart-warming. Their dogs' new behavior blew their minds.

Next, I suggested that they keep a leash on the dogs as much as possible during the next week, but not 100 percent of the time. "Don't eliminate off-leash playtime, and you don't need to leash them at night or when you go out."

"We must always view things from Digby and Jersey's point of view. They perceive that the leash connection means they need to keep track of you. If you get up and move around your home for any reason, they are obligated to react and follow you. This naturally positions you guys higher on your Leader Ladders and makes the dogs subservient to you both. Posturing or establishing pack position is primal for all canines. When you seize the highest pack position from them, they will be relegated to a lower ranking. Digby and Jersey will be much happier as balanced dogs. This will result in their respecting and trusting you, which has not been the case until now. This alone will make the future very positive versus the bleak outlook you had before today."

Both David and Susan were beaming with excitement and confidence. They also realized the commitment required.

"I'm looking forward to seeing you next Sunday", I said. "I am expecting great results from all four of you. I know that you will be focused on your objective; to have two balanced dogs while creating a safe environment for your new baby." I gave them a business card and told them to call me if they had any questions.

## **Children as Pack Leaders; They have mini Leader Ladders**

The relationship between dogs and children is very different than between dogs and adults. Age is obviously a huge factor with children. There's a wide spectrum of ability between children of all ages. Kids develop both physically and mentally very differently, so their age is not necessarily a qualification when it comes to dog training.

When I worked with Michael, a well-known athlete, and his family, I mentioned to his wife, Diane, that their seven-year-old daughter, Sara, might not be able to handle a couple of hours of me talking about canine behavior. I was not, however, concerned about their 14-year-old daughter, Alex.

Diane told me that her youngest, Sara, would likely be the one to stay focused because she was the most involved with their dog, Rosie.

Indeed, Alex showed very little interest during that first visit. In fact, she was rather indifferent to my lessons. Sara was intently focused on the whole process, resulting in positioning herself high on her own Leader Ladder. Michael came home near the end of my visit. As he gave Rosie the usual excited welcome, Sara instantly corrected him and told him about the new and improved way of entering the home.

See? I got that one all wrong. The bottom line; when it comes to the age factor, it's up to each parent to decide and consciously monitor.

Usually, the younger the child, the more volatile and emotional their behavior can be. A young child may get angry with a dog if he doesn't behave exactly like he wants the dog to. This can result in the child hurting the dog or vice versa. The major concern is that dogs read energy with Superman-like ability. If a child is angry and/or frustrated their dog will know this, and likely show dominance over the child. It is hard enough for adults to control their own energy, so the maturity level of a child is crucial. Most dogs welcome the soft tenderness of a child, but not unpredictable outbursts.

If a child is mature enough to understand this and can control himself, then he is capable of climbing his own Leader Ladder. If he is too young to reach this level, then a parent or older sibling can share their Leader Ladder with them.

With the proper supervision, you can encourage your child to play by the rules of the Game of Canine. If you are working with a young child, together you could give the dog a 'Sit' command by both saying, "Sit," simultaneously. This would seem like fun to your child because the dog obeyed his/her command, even though the dog more likely responded to you, the parent. Instruct the child to give the command with authority. It's not a request; "Please sit." It's an order; "Private Canine, sit." Both the child and parent can also include a hand signal while giving a verbal command to increase the effectiveness of the child in the process. I promote double-communication as often as possible, utilizing both audio and visual senses.

With time, you should slowly, progressively pass the wand of control over to your child. Next, have the child give a voice command, accompanied by a hand signal, while you only whisper the command as well as give a hand signal. Next, you can make the hand signal with minimal movement, not a full motion, without saying the command, so that in essence, the dog would be obeying the child.

Eventually the child could give the complete message while you're simply standing nearby. Slowly develop this process to the point where you are not in the same room as the dog and child, but within earshot in case the dog doesn't obey the child. If this should happen, you should enter the room with the energy of a freight train, and have the child repeat the command using both voice and hand signals, but with more authority on their part. Between your burst of energy and a repeated message from the child, the dog is likely to obey. Then wait for about 10 seconds and have the child praise and reward her with a treat, as this was the original command given.

As kids become more confident, they are able to deal with dogs much more effectively because they have a better understanding of how to maintain calm, strong, green-ring energy. Always be aware of a child's energy. They can be calm one minute and screaming the next. This sharing of power with a child is a long-term project. As odd as this may sound, the slower you progress, the faster the dog learns. Master each step before proceeding to the next level of learning. This will avoid one step forward and two steps backward. A balanced, respectful relationship will develop between the dog and child, as the child climbs up the Leader Ladder, whether they are sharing a Leader Ladder or are establishing a ranking on their own. The better they follow The Recipe, the more they act in a black or white way – the better their pack position.

Posturing is paramount and automatic for canines. They don’t have an off-switch when it comes to pack posturing – be it with a child or adult.

**Bringing a Newborn Home; the new king or queen**

Newborn babies can be introduced to dogs safely and effectively. Mothers are typically not kept in the hospital more than a day or two. I suggest that the father bring home a soiled diaper and a sleeper, as both will carry the baby's scent. The diaper should not be given to the dog as a toy, just to smell. Let the dog come close but do not let him touch the diaper. Her nose 'knows' from afar. You can also put the sleeper in the dog's bed, so she can sleep with the scent. The idea is to acclimatize the dog to the new scent. If time permits, you can repeat this with another sleeper and diaper before the newborn is brought home.

When the baby and mom arrive home, I suggest that Dad wait in the car with baby for a few minutes while Mom goes into the home to greet the dog. After all, she has been gone for a couple of days, and the dog will likely be super excited to see her. Mom – be sure to let the dog settle and show respect before acknowledging her. This will also give the dog a chance to associate the baby's scent on you. Settle or calm the dog before Dad brings in Junior. Use a leash if necessary to keep control – control is imperative at this juncture.

The baby must be considered a new king or queen of the pack from this point forward. Once the baby is in the house and everyone is calm and settled (especially the dog), let the dog come close for a smell, but not too close. This is your space and not the dog's. This area must be viewed as the *leader's circle*. No followers are allowed just yet. Establish this boundary and control this space emphatically. This is not a baby, *per se*, it is a new leader in the pack and must be respected as such. The pack posture of the baby is paramount.

As you hold your child, give the dog some simple obedience commands, which will create another scenario for you to praise and/or treat her, cementing a positive relationship between dog and child. These commands will be coming from both the parent and baby at the same time, which positions the baby with you on your Leader Ladder. Never let the dog into the baby's room. Make her wait and watch from the doorway. She must be respectful of this boundary. (This lesson should be taught well before the birth of the baby and then practiced and reinforced afterward.) As the baby is changed and the dog watches patiently from the doorway, praise and treat her.

The period that you wait before allowing your dog to get next to the baby will depend on the level of confidence you have in your dog. Every situation and every dog is different, based on the dog's level of balance. Even though I am sure you know this, I feel that I must emphasize: *Never* leave a dog and child of any age together unattended. I believe that I could safely leave Satchmo unattended in a nursery with babies crawling on the floor, but I would *never* consider it. Always take either the dog or baby with you whenever you leave the room. My favorite question is most appropriate in this situation: "When did I give up control?" Answer, "I didn't." Proactive management will avoid any regrets.

While outside walking with the baby and dog, keep her beside you and not in front or off to the side, like in an imaginary box. This is known as the heel position. As this takes place, the stroller will be ahead, therefore, it is the baby leading the hunt/walk, which distinguishes your baby as a leader. Never tie the leash to a stroller, in case the dog decides to chase a squirrel or anything else that she might run after. This would only result in a stroller being tipped over or worse, e.g., getting dragged onto the road. By having the leash in your hand, not wrapped around your hand, you will have independent control of the dog, autonomous of the stroller. With a leash wrapped around your hand, if your dog's innate predator/prey drive kicks in and he starts to chase something, it's difficult to let go of the leash to avoid getting dragged around, especially if your dog is strong. It would be devastating if he pulled hard enough to make you let go of the stroller, especially if the ground is not level and the stroller rolled away on its own.

If you are fortunate enough to have a balanced, obedient dog, all of what I suggest above will not be an issue. The dog's mindset will be to obey and serve you as her leader. If, however, your dog is not balanced and frequently shows dominant, protective behavior, it is wise to seek professional assistance. I am often asked, "When is the best time to retain your services?" My answer is always; "A week before you bring a dog into your home. This way you won't develop bad habits, only good ones." Another answer would be, "A week before you bring a newborn baby home."

I relate this to learning how to play golf. Is it better to take professional lessons at the very beginning or wait until you have developed a major slice in your swing? It's obviously advantageous to learn to play with the assistance of a pro from the get-go. By the time most people call me, they have owned their dog for some time and bad habits are prevalent. I can't imagine anything more important than the need to have a balanced dog when there are young children in the home. *We can't change yesterday, but we can control today and tomorrow.*

The second-best time to engage a professional's services is immediately. Don't wait. Be proactive and not reactive to a negative situation. Children cannot protect themselves. That is a parent's job.

## Summary

It is imperative to use forethought and to be proactive when dogs and children are together. Consider my favorite question; "When did I give up control?" The answer must be: "I didn't, because I was fanatical about the safety of the children." Negative things can happen when we don't pay enough attention to any situation involving children and dogs. The mandate is that all members of the family (age is irrelevant) must be perceived as pack leaders by your dog.

When a newborn baby enters the home, the parameters must be established from the start. By allowing your dog near (but not too close to or touching) the baby, boundaries are immediately created. Teach your dog to sit and watch from the doorway of the baby's room whenever you are in the room. Don't exclude your dog from the baby – just not too close. The dog's priority is simply to smell the baby. Include your dog, from a controlled, short distance from the baby. Complete exclusion may create a negative response. Be acutely aware of her body language and sense of respect for the situation. *Never* leave the baby and dog alone together for even a few seconds. Take your dog or baby with you.

Eventually, as your confidence increases, allow the dog closer until she closely sniffs and touches the baby's clothes with her nose, but not the baby's face. Of course, the dog must be calm always whenever near the baby. Even a friendly paw can seriously injure the baby. The rate of progression until a dog is allowed close enough to touch the baby will vary with each dog. As always, it is better to progress slowly versus too quickly. It is not mandatory for all dogs to get close enough to touch the baby.

All children in the home must position themselves on a Leader Ladder, be it their own or a shared one with an older sibling or adult. A parent or sibling can act as a co-leader with a child, by giving the dog a command together, simultaneously. As your dog gets used to the tandem commands, you can transfer the leadership role to your child by standing a short distance away as the child gives the dog commands. If your dog disobeys a command, both you and your child can clap your hands, say, "Hey", and step into the dog's space. Repeat the command together to send a double message. Progressively increase the distance from the child as they give the dog commands, until the dog consistently obeys your child. This way your child will be manning their own Leader Ladder.

All training with dogs must be established on a progressive basis. Dogs cannot jump steps. They must take each step one-at-a-time. After all, we wouldn't expect a child in Grade 1 piano to play Mozart. I believe the slower you train a dog the faster they learn; within reason. Wait until each level has been mastered before advancing to the next stage.

The main consideration with children, of all ages, is that they are perceived to be pack leaders by your dog. The principal of this book is to teach humans to think like dogs, hence, to be able to see things from the canine viewpoint. Children are extremely vulnerable, and it is the obligation of a parent to ensure their safety when around dogs. The best way to do this is to have a balanced dog who respects all the humans in the pack, who are higher on the Leader Ladder.

It is the job of a parent to protect the child from the dog … as well as the dog from the child.

# Chapter 24

## Six Ways to Interrupt Negative Behavior

*Use their system, not ours.*

One exceptionally busy morning at the dog park, I found it almost impossible to be productive. There was an inordinate amount of activity producing an irritating amount of noise, which made it difficult to focus on my chores. The number of dogs running around set an attendance record, at least when I was there. Add to this, another record was being set; the most kids in the park at one time. To top this off, there were droves of parents yelling at either dogs or kids, trying to keep things under control. All of this created a whirlwind of commotion throughout the park.

Some parents were remarkably calm and successful at keeping both their dogs and children out of trouble. Others were totally irresponsible concerning their kids, dogs or both. Dog behavior is a mirror reflection of owner behavior. This was most evident with parents who had no control and who were yelling or screaming at their dogs *and* kids.

My ability to focus on my work proved to be *mission impossible*, so I sat with Satchmo under our usual shade tree at the top of the small hill, trying to escape the insanity down by the creek. Several dogs ran up to check us out only to discover our inactivity, which was not very appealing to them. They immediately returned to the serious action. Even though Satchmo would have loved to join in the activity below, I didn't want him getting into any trouble. A dog fight could occur at any time with this number of dogs interacting, especially when unbalanced dogs were not supervised. My volunteer job description clearly does not include being a referee at a dog fight.

I noticed an older couple walking across the parking lot. They had a dog, who was appropriately leashed, with them. This handsome dog was a German Short Haired Pointer. The couple didn't let her loose when they passed through the second security gate (all dog parks have two gates to pass through to assist in keeping control of dogs) which was a good idea because of her constant pulling and barking. Her dominant behavior could easily set off an aggressive reaction from some of the other dogs.

The couple seemed to be searching for someone, who turned out to be me. They made their way up the hill towards us. If there was ever a time that you would wish your dog *would* pull, it would be while walking uphill. The dog was pulling the lady like a Clydesdale. Upon their arrival at the hill top and still out of breath, they attempted to get their dog under control with very little success. The score was unofficially 5-0 for the Pointer. Eventually they achieved minimal control of their dog, enough that we could carry on a conversation, even though she was constantly tugging on the leash. This earned her another point in the game. It was 6-1 for the dog. She was fixated on pulling toward Satchmo, who was alertly sitting and waiting for me to release him.

Hal and Adrienne introduced themselves, along with Rags. They mentioned that another couple from their church, who were dog whispering clients of mine, had recommended me to them, and had mentioned that I was always here on Sunday mornings. They told me they had given up going to church that morning hoping to see me. Next, the conversation turned to Rags and her many problems.

"Short of aggression", Hal said, "Rags has every misbehavior that you have listed in your dog whisperer brochure. We have tried several dog-training programs, but she still acts like a wild beast. Sometimes, if we have a treat, she will be obedient and act like an angel when we are alone in our house with no distractions. She can be very loving and a wonderful companion. However, when outside it's like a switch goes off in her head and we cannot control her, even if we hold up cheese, her favorite treat. It is like she is possessed. She won't listen. She tugs on the leash like a tow truck. She goes nuts whenever other dogs, cats, squirrels or any other animals are within view. She constantly jumps on people with excitement. She becomes a Dr. Jekyll and Mrs. Hyde dog whenever we leave our house, versus the quiet, loving dog that we get to enjoy when indoors.

Our friend told us about your 90:10 rule: 90 percent of the time Rags is great and 10 percent of the time we're not sure if we want to scream or pull out our hair. Bruce, can you help us? We are at our wits end."

I could hear the stress and emotion in Hal's voice. Suddenly, Adrienne exploded and yelled at Rags, simultaneously pulling her leash firmly. I watched Rags as Adrienne let out a scream of commands. Rags' demeanour changed in a heartbeat. She stopped pulling, stood calmly with her ears back, and looked up at Adrienne. I think she was shocked and didn't know how to react.

"Well done", I said. "She finally settled down."

Both Hal and Adrienne looked a little surprised at my congratulatory praise.

"Look at the results that you just achieved in a few seconds", I said. "You exploded and interrupted her negative behavior and redirected her thoughts to you. Nice job."

I explained that the objective of behavioral management is to interrupt negative behavior and praise positive behavior. I then suggested that she praise Rags for being calm, so that Rags knew what behavior pleased Adrienne. By continuously acknowledging calm behavior with a praise, touch, and/or a treat, Rags will be encouraged to repeat the behavior. I explained the concept of the Game of Canine and pointed out the huge point that Adrienne had just scored. It was a game-changer in Rags' mind. I also explained about calm, strong, green-ring energy. If Adrienne had gotten the same results with green-ring energy, the point scored would have been of better quality.

At that very moment I tuned into Mr. Satchmo's whining. He, understandably, wanted to come and meet Rags. I looked his way and simply said, "Hey", while putting my hand up, indicating for him to go calm. He stopped whining as he lowered his ears and stared at me with those heartbreaking, sad eyes, trying to convince me to change my mind. I'm only a sucker for the pleading eyes of a child.

I used this opportunity to explain the interruption process. Based on the core of the Game of Canine, C*ontrol the calm to win the game* is the only way for humans to score points. Unbelievably, Rags remained quiet, calm and respectful. Hal mentioned that it would normally be impossible to get Rags this calm. I again suggested that Adrienne show her pleasure with Rags' positive, calm behavior. This would be an ideal time to pet her and give her a treat. Hal had a treat out of his pocket in a flash as he started to approach Rags. This prompted her to excitedly start moving toward him while her enjoyable, calm behavior dissipated. I suggested that Adrienne give the leash a correctional pop, step in front of Rags and quietly and sternly say, "Sit", along with giving her an assertive stare. This worked dramatically as Rags showed immediate respect by sitting and looking up to Adrienne.

"Wow", Adrienne said with a smile.

I suggested that Adrienne, not Hal, give Rags a touch and a treat, but not for about ten seconds. If a dog obeys a 'sit' command it is ideal to praise immediately. However, if she doesn't obey your 'sit' command and it is necessary for you to be assertive, say by stepping into her space/face, it is critical to wait for her short term memory bank to fill with calm sitting, or the next time you tell her to sit, she will likely wait until you step into her space/face, because that is what she perceives she was praised for in the past. I said, "After about a ten second wait, praise the exact behavior you wanted, her calmly sitting." I added, "*He who has the leash is in control.* If someone else gives her commands she will be confused as to which person she should respond to."

This short lesson on interruption was impactful to their pack. Adrienne and Hal suddenly had a new level of control. I explained to them several methods of interruption (for a more complete list, see below), which would result in Rags stopping whatever she was doing and calmly redirecting her focus to them. I included a description of calm, strong, green-ring leader-energy. Even though Adrienne exploded and resorted to yelling … OK, screaming … at Rags, this got very positive results. The mandate in the future would be to attain the same results using calm, green-ring energy. That is why I'm called a dog whisperer and not a dog yeller. Lastly, I suggested they increase Rags' exercise time to burn off her exuberant excitement.

It was extremely rewarding for me to witness the immediate transformation of their pack from chaos to relative calm. All members seemed noticeably happy as they made their way to the parking lot. Rags was not pulling like before, perhaps slightly but with considerably less vigor. I smiled as I replayed in my mind the crazy out-of-control dog that I originally met as she towed Adrienne up the hill, compared to the new and improved model. Rags didn't even react to all the commotion of the other park patrons, four-legged or two-legged. I looked forward to meeting them in the weeks to come, so that I could witness their continued progress.

## Dog Whisperer Lesson; six levels of interruption

Negative behavior can come in many forms and degrees. Say a dog is given a basic 'sit/stay' command and a short while later decides to move a little closer to you. Many people would likely consider this minimally bad behavior. However, it would be considered negative, since he disobeyed or broke the command given. At the other end of the spectrum, a dog could be excessively barking, jumping, lunging or biting people or dogs.

The objective when interrupting negative behavior is to have the dog stop whatever they are doing and redirect their attention to you. This results in a calm dog, waiting for your direction. I know that I have repeated this mantra, but it is the backbone of what I teach; *Control the calm to win the game.* When interrupting negative behavior, *less is best.* This means that whispering is more impactful than yelling. If you quietly speak in a whisper on a regular basis, then your dog will be more likely to keep track of you. If you constantly yell, a dog will tend to tune you out and your message will be diluted, just like with kids.

I know that when I'm with Satchmo, most people do not hear me give him a command, even if they are close by. My verbal messages to him are whispers and are typically accompanied by a soft whistle sound and/or a hand signal. This means that he always must be cognizant of me. If he misses the command because of other noises or distractions, then I increase the level of my message. If I need to raise my voice and say his name when he is being impish and not obeying me, he knows that I am taking things up a notch, and he usually reacts immediately. When I don't get the result I am looking for, I usually approach him and step into his space so that I physically make my presence felt. At this point he is likely looking up at me, and if I thought that he didn't hear me the first time, I would either give him a whisper, a hand signal or a very quiet whistle command. Remember the Golden Rule; *"Tell him once and never take no for an answer."*

In my experience, there are six levels of interruption. No. 1 is the lowest level, while No. 6 is the maximum. The first four of these interruption techniques requires a quick explosive response. The last two on the list simulate the physical behavior of canines.

We all know how a dog can change from being totally calm to full excitement or aggression, in a split-second. This instantaneous change of behavior is explosive. An example is when a calm dog is lying down and you pick up their leash or use the *walk* word. Their split-second, explosive reaction is to spring onto their feet, anticipating that they are going for a walk. Another example is explosive aggressive barking if the doorbell rings. Our reaction to their misbehavior must implement various levels of explosive interruptions.

A tiny explosion is a snap of our fingers, a clap or a quick correctional pop of a leash. All are meant to redirect a dog's focus to us. (For more details, see below.) Other times we may need to explode with much more vigor. A very frustrated client once called me because his Chihuahua regularly soiled beside his chair, both indoors and out. I asked how he'd reacted to the last incident. He told me that he scolded the dog by saying, "No, no, no", and escorted her outside. I asked him if I had ever used the word explosion. He responded, "Many times". I then told him that I was going to put the phone down on my desk and demonstrate how I would have *explosively* reacted to such a situation. I jumped up while assertively saying, "Hey", and clapping loudly. I then proceeded to, hypothetically, chase her down my hallway while clapping at her as she ran off. I returned to my office, picked up the phone and asked him, "What color is my ring?"

He responded, "Obviously green. You sound quite calm. I guess that my explosions need to be a whole lot bigger to make my point that I am the leader of this pack."

"The fact that your dog continues to misbehave and soil beside you definitely requires a more significant response from you", I said. "Remember that, unlike in the human world where respect is *earned*, in the canine world respect is *taken*. Also remember to give your dog lots of praise when she is behaving the way you like."

When interrupting all misbehaviors, be cognizant of utilizing green-ring energy. A light, sharp clap or an explosive 'Hey' sound can be at a low volume and still get great results. No yelling or anger, just a simple light explosion to get her attention. Less is best, but if a bigger response is necessary, due to a more serious situation, then increase the intensity proportionately.

## The six levels of interruption

The **first** level of interruption is simply with a little sound of, "Hey". It is sharp and quick. Try saying it softly, but sharply. That doesn't mean that you can't yell if a serious situation requires it.

I remember working with a woman, named Angela, who owned a Portuguese Water Dog. It was our second session, and she was showing me how well her dog, Harley, had progressed while walking down the street. Every time she stopped, she yelled, “Hey”, at a volume that made me jump. A man cutting his grass across the street heard her yelling over the noise of his power lawnmower. I suggested to Angela that she should only whisper to Harley from then on. She tried it and Harley was brilliant.

The **second** level of interruption is to clap your hands. This can be soft or hard, whatever is necessary. Again, the objective is to have your dog stop whatever he is doing and redirect his thoughts and focus to you. It is impossible to make the sound of a clap last very long. The only variance is how hard you clap. It is possible to use interruptions No. 1 and 2 simultaneously. Say, “Hey”, as you clap. This intensifies your interruption.

The **third** level of interruption is to pop the leash. This is a very short, correctional pop. The leash is a fabulous tool to communicate to your dog. The best word I know to describe the brevity of a pop is a musical term, *staccato*. This is a musical note with a dot above it. (You would expect a guy with a dog named Satchmo, Louis Armstrong’s nickname, to be musically inclined.) If we snap our fingers, the sound would last for only a split second. A pop should last about the same length of time. If you hold the leash tight, even for half a second, it would be a pull and not a pop. You should be able to lightly pop the leash with a four-pound Chihuahua and not lift their front feet off the ground. Think *staccato* or *infinitesimal*.

I use the leash pop for three different reasons. If you use the pop very lightly, it becomes the norm. If you need to increase the intensity, then you can. There are three distinct directions of a pop:

1. Straight upward gives the message to sit. This slight connection tells the dog to move in the direction of a sit. If he doesn't sit then help him out by adding the word, "Sit", and move in front, facing him. Get close into his space, with his snout touching your legs. This makes your dog feel your presence and increase the effectiveness of the command. If he then sits, wait ten seconds and give him a huge praise along with a treat if you have one handy.

2. Straight back indicates that you are stopping while on a walk, with your arm extended straight down. It only needs to be a wiggle or a light flick of the leash to indicate that you are stopping. I often combine this with a very soft 'Hey' sound to enhance my communication. If he is tardy while stopping and tries to move slightly ahead of you, then repeat the rearward pop with a little enhanced firmness. He must walk respectfully beside and not in front of you.

3. Give a pop sideways, parallel to the ground, to unbalance him. If, say, he stands up on you, this sideways pop unbalances him and redirects him off you. If he doesn't get down, repeat the pop and increase the firmness each time, until he leaves on his own. In no time he will respond to a very light sideways pop. Often people push a dog off when he stands up on them. The idea is for the dog to make the decision to get down on his own, just as he decided to jump up. If he goes in front of you while walking, you could give a sideways pop to unbalance him and then do an about-face. He then must turn and catch

up to you. This is a very effective method to eliminate his walking in front. When this turnaround procedure is repeated several times in a row, he will likely be totally focused on you.

By using the leash to give various pops to your dog, the level of communication and connection between you is increased exponentially. The levels of a pop can range from a slight wiggle of the leash to being strong enough to tip the dog off balance. This is obviously relative to the size of your dog and seriousness of a situation. The No. 1 and 3 ways to interrupt can be given together as well. A 'Hey' sound, along with a slight pop, is a double command; using both audio and physical to intensify your message.

The **fourth** level of interruption is more physical. When two canines, wolves or dogs, fight or wrestle playfully, they tend to nip or bite each other in two specific areas, e.g., the neck and belly. Both areas are bite zones to canines. The specific neck area that I am referring to is at *10 o'clock and 2 o'clock* on the throat. It is the same spot that human's use to take their pulse, upward at the soft spot beside the windpipe. The belly area is behind the ribs and in front of the hind leg. It is a soft area where wild canines bite to open-up an animal that they have killed, to get to the organs in the stomach.

By touching or tapping these spots you can simulate how canines nip or bite each other. It is designed to surprise or shock them slightly, which gets them to focus on you. (Imagine someone coming up behind you and giving you a light poke in the ribs. You would jump with a surprised or shocked look on your face as you turned around to see who was there.) I don't bother touching dogs elsewhere on their body because of how effective both areas are. Some dogs are more sensitive in one area than the other. If you find this to be the case, then use it to your advantage. All it will likely take is a touch.

I once worked with a Bernese Mountain Dog that, while outdoors, was extremely aggressive with both dogs and cats. I tapped her in the belly area when she reacted aggressively to a passing cat. She got riled up and showed her dislike by growling, snarling and rearing up. I said to the owners, "That was awesome". They looked at me like I was crazy. I then added, "I just found her sensitive spot … just like some people are far more ticklish then others." From then on I only had to touch this spot for her to respond by looking at me and giving me her full attention. In this case, one tap was good for life.

You can also lightly press one of the bite zones in the throat area to help keep a dog's focus on you. If, say, a dog is approaching, and your dog will likely react with either uncontrollable excitement or aggression, try pressing a finger or thumb in the throat bite zone, before he reacts. This proactive management will connect the two of you and will help him remain calm.

The **fifth** level of interruption is to put your hand on your dog's throat, touching both bite zones on the neck at the same time. I call it a double bite or a kill bite, as canines in the wild tear open the throat of their prey to finish a kill. Usually a light touch is all that is needed because of the sensitivity of this area. If the negative behavior is serious or maybe aggressive, then I would give a light squeeze. If the aggression indicates the possibility of someone being bitten, I would also, simultaneously, grab the dog by the scruff with my other hand for maximum control.

One day, while I was giving a clinic in a pet store, a local newspaper photographer came to take some pictures of the event. He asked me if I could gather all the dogs present under the store's sign. I had all the dogs sitting respectfully except Marmaduke, the Great Dane, who was young and stubborn. He refused to sit so I gave him a double bite. As soon as I touched his neck, without even closing my fingers, he sat and went calm instantly. His owner was behind me and expressed her astonishment at how he went calm and sat so quickly. "How did you do that?" she asked. I told her that I touched his neck, and he immediately responded. This is a kill-zone for both canines and humans. Have someone put their hand lightly on your throat to feel the effect this has.

Satchmo responds to the kill-bite immediately. If I give him a tap in the belly or neck, as described in the fourth way to interrupt, he is oblivious. There's no effect whatsoever. If he is being impish, I only need to put my hand ever so lightly on his throat. He reacts by freezing and focusing directly at me. When you know what your dog reacts to best, then use it to give yourself an edge.

The last or **sixth** level of interruption is to either pin a dog on the ground or grab their scruff to lift their front feet off the ground. This is certainly the highest level of interruption and should not be overused, as there is no greater or more forceful way to interrupt. I only use this method for two distinct reasons.

1. If a dog is being insubordinate and just won't listen. There may have been a buildup to his insubordination, over a period of time, as he was constantly challenging you. An insubordinate pack member in a wild canine pack would likely receive a similar action but with much more intensity. We would use the word vicious to describe this response.

2. If a dog is showing aggression to people or dogs, and just won't stop. Snarling, biting, snapping or growling that the dog won't stop warrants either pinning them down or lifting their front feet off the ground.

If the dog is small this is a very simple procedure. Hold them by the back of the neck, up high, just below their ears, and push their chin to the floor/ground or lift them by the scruff until their front feet, or all four feet, are off the ground. Hold them until they go calm. This usually happens within a few seconds, but not always. If they are fighting, squirming or squealing, then hold them securely until they stop. The screaming is their way of saying, "I don't want to be held or dominated." This does not hurt, it only controls them. The lift-off-the-ground looks like it hurts but it does not. Their mother used to carry them by the scruff.

If the dog is a larger breed, then get one or two handfuls of scruff. That's the skin on the top of their neck, just below their ears. Next, roll your hands toward you, not away from you, and at the same time quickly pull your dog off balance. This will cause him to tip sideways into a prone position. Hold onto their scruff until he calms down. This may seem drastic or hurtful. Drastic yes – hurtful no. This is the canine way of totally dominating each other.

I once watched a documentary on wolves. A mother was teaching her pups to fish. Three of the four pups, about a year old, were having a feast eating the plentiful salmon swimming up-river. The fourth pup was having no part of it and refused to go into the water. The mother grabbed him by the scruff with her mouth, pinned him on the ground and growled at him. Next, she nipped him in the belly bite-zone area. He immediately walked straight into the river. His insubordination was not tolerated and was physically (not hurtfully) dealt with. My mission is to simulate the same process, with no malice, anger or pain in any way.

The above six ways to interrupt negative behavior are all designed to stop dogs from whatever they are doing and calmly redirect their focus to you. Remember that 'less is best', but use whatever level is needed. Do not overuse No. 6. Also; *Never take no for an answer.* You're the General – They're the Privates.

## **Summary**

A basic principal in the Game of Canine is to interrupt negative behavior and praise positive, calm behavior. *Control the calm to win the game*. The mandate is to redirect the dog's focus to you. It's not mandatory for your dog to look at you, provided he stops whatever he's doing and connects with you mentally. Say, he is barking at something and you give him a clap sound. The objective is for him to stop barking. If he stops barking but is still looking in the same direction, this would be considered a victory. I frequently say, "Looking is free". If your next command is, "Come", then he would be expected to approach you. The severity of the negative behavior will dictate the level of interruption required. There are six distinct methods of interruption (explained above) that can be used to redirect your dog's focus.

It is much more effective to be proactive versus reactive. If you can anticipate negative behavior before it happens, then control is easily maintained. When this happens, a quiet and simple 'Hey' sound will likely suffice. This will bring your dog's focus to you, causing him to disconnect from what he was about to do. As soon as you become his focal point, don't forget to praise his good behavior. We cannot always be proactive, but when we must react to the negative behavior, the appropriate level of interruption should be utilized. Remember; *less is best*. Be as light as possible, both verbally and physically, while interrupting your dog.

## Chapter 25

## Backyard Perimeter Barking

*Border patrol is a human job.*

Whitney, with her two Boxers, arrived at the dog park one chilly but bright sunny morning, only to be greeted by a ruckus before they even got through the front gate. A female Bulldog inside the fence was not in a welcoming mood. She was trying to scare off all four-legged comers. Of course, both Boxers reacted by aggressively barking back at the Bulldog. I stood up to take in the circus and witnessed all three dogs running back and forth along the fence line as they tried to see which side could out-bark the other. The Boxers, Jazz and Raven, gave up the verbal battle first, but continued bouncing dominantly along the fence line. Whitney finally got control of her dogs by using a very loud, angry voice. In other words, she was screaming at the top of her lungs.

I tried to ignore the conflict, anticipating that both owners would be responsible and de-escalate the situation. I got that wrong. Whitney was unable to enter the park because the Bulldog was allowed to continue barking, which only fueled the situation. I was somewhat taken aback by how long the Bulldog's owner stood and watched the charade without any intervention at all. She just kept talking to another owner, with no regard to the aggravation being caused by her boisterous dog. Whitney had full control of both Jazz and Raven, so the Bulldog had very little to complain about. One would have thought that the Bulldog would eventually cease and desist. This didn't happen until

Whitney yelled to the owner, “Excuse me, lady. Please get please control of your dog”.

The self-involved, narcissistic, disrespectful dog owner stopped chatting and began, ever so slowly, to walk toward her dog, Bella. All the while she was giving Whitney a long, indignant stare. As she did, she inadvertently stepped in the sloppy dog poop Bella had deposited earlier. It didn’t go well with her stylish, very thin-soled sandals. She freaked out. The mess was not only on the bottom of her sandals; it was oozing between her toes.

I was hard pressed to contain my composure and not laugh out loud. After all, it was hilarious. After rubbing her sandal on the grass, still in a fit of rage, she leashed Bella and walked over to the tap area where I was working. I don’t think I’ll ever forget the expression on her face as she tried to wash the mess. She didn’t make eye contact with me, nor utter a single word. Then she marched, red-faced and embarrassed, back to her car as Bella wailed and barked at the Boxers.

“Peace and quiet at last”, I said out loud to myself. Whitney walked around the park for a short while before she arrived at where I was working to attach a new hose. The old hose had been chewed through enough times that it was too short to be of much good. It always amazes me how some owners are oblivious to where their dog is and what they are doing at a leash-free park. I guess, to some owners, that also means responsibility-free.

Jazz and Raven wandered over my way to see what I was up to, closely followed by Whitney, who stopped to chat. I turned on the water to check for any leaks. Satchmo was at his best. He sat attentively and resisted his desire to approach the Boxers, even though his rump was in a constant state of motion. The Boxers were quite thirsty, so their primary focus was getting a drink. They both enthusiastically lapped up water from the hose and I could picture a major slobbery mess on the kitchen floor every time they took a drink. The water endlessly poured from their mouths as they walked away toward Satchmo. At this time, I gave Satchmo the OK to leave his post and mingle. They seemed to get along immediately. It was game-on for the three of them.

Whitney talked about the behavior of her dogs at the fence, before the lady removed her Bulldog. She was conscious and concerned that her dogs were uncontrollable and that their negative behavior had been embarrassing. "This is the same behavior I see every time I let them out into the yard. They run along the fence line, barking like they are possessed. This whole routine amplifies, and they become obsessive if our neighbour's Husky is outside. The crazy part is that all three dogs get along great when they are in the front yard while on leashes. Bryce, the Husky, is friendly with both Jazz and Raven. It seems that all three of them forget their training and manners when they are running along their respective fence lines. Something primal takes over. To hear the three of them carry on, one would think that they were in the midst of a dog war."

To me this explained how well they engaged with Satchmo. They had no perimeters to protect.

I asked Whitney if she had a few minutes, so that I could explain how to combat this perimeter ritual that she was living with.

She was all ears. I said, "First of all, you did a very commendable job containing and controlling your boys while outside the fence. You had them calm in short order. Even though you were shrieking as loudly as they were barking, the result was that you won by calming them." I talked her through some basics of the Game of Canine, highlighting the importance of green-ring energy. I said, "Screaming is not green-ring energy".

I described a simple course of action to take when her dogs are let outside. I said to her, "Your main objective is to take away Jazz and Raven's job of being on-duty while outside. It must become your job, from their mindset, to act as the border patrol, not theirs. I suggest that you keep them on a leash as you take them out to the yard. Start when Bryce is not out in his yard. This will simplify your mission to control the perimeter. Calmly walk around the outside of your yard, as close to the fence line or garden as possible. It is not necessary to walk through the garden or between the shrubs and the fence. I would walk back and forth around the yard four or five times. This puts you in charge of the perimeter, not them."

"Once the perimeter walk is complete, stop at their *hot spot*, the place where they get the most vocal and aggressive with Bryce. The objective is to get *a calm* here, before you unleash them. By overcoming their angst at the hot spot, all other areas in the yard should be easy to maintain control. Once unleashed, they should casually walk away while sniffing the area. If, however, they start to get fixated on the fence line then re-leash the perpetrator(s) and repeat the border patrol walk a couple more times before you once again calmly remove the leash. Repeat this, over and over, until they get it and calmly walk away from you."

"As you repeat this process every time they go outside over the next few days, without Bryce's presence, they will accept you taking over the perimeter patrol. This sounds easier than it is. You will have to repeat the perimeter walk over and over to effectively get your point across that *you* are the new border-patrol-leader. They will get the picture as you continuously dominate them throughout the whole process. You must be consistent, calm and strong while never taking *no* for an answer. Take charge and lead them, 'Oh great alpha border-patrol-leader'."

"Next, ramp up the intensity for them and keep them calm while Bryce is in his yard. Make sure that you walk the perimeter with them before stopping where Bryce likely will be enthusiastically barking through the fence. It will be a game-winning test for you to maintain a calm. Only a calm owner can have a calm dog. Think green-ring calm. You may want to try this with one dog at a time to increase the odds of success. Only release Jazz and Raven if they remain calm. Once again, the mission is for them to calmly walk away from Bryce and just sniff around your yard. Just as you won the game when entering the park today with the Bulldog, your mission is to get the same result when it is Bryce doing the barking on the other side of the fence at home. Eventually you will want to be able to let them out on their own while Bryce is out next door. This will be the last hurdle for you all to overcome. Remember, everything is progressive with dogs; take your time."

Whitney was very appreciative of what I suggested and seemed keen on putting it into practice. She promised that she would check in for a progress report in the coming weeks.

**Dog Whisperer Story; two out-of-control Westies**

A young couple once called me about major barking issues they were having with their two West Highland White Terriers, or Westies. It seemed that they had a triangle of a problem. They lived in a new subdivision next to a very popular public pathway, which led to the park at the back of their yard. In addition, their neighbour on the opposite side of their yard had a boisterous Old English Sheep dog, named Sam. It was impossible to enjoy any quiet time in their yard or back porch if Stella and Abby were outside with them. Even inside the house it was impossible to keep the dogs from barking at anything they could see or hear outside.

Janet and Bob had been one of the first couples to purchase a house in the new survey, well before any of the homes were built, and they certainly didn't anticipate how busy the park or pathway would be. Add the unexpected dog living next door and *voilà* you have a quagmire of problems. Any one of the areas might be manageable, but compounded, the situation was exasperating. The pathway was like a main street because it was the only shortcut from the survey to the park behind their house. All other routes to the park required a three-block walk around the neighbourhood. When Janet called, all I could hear in the background was barking or yelling by all pack members, two-legged and four-legged, as they jostled for power.

I arrived at their home on a Thursday evening. Bob came out to greet me as I pulled into the driveway. He wanted to warn me about what I was about to walk into. He was concerned that I wouldn't be able to handle a couple of small boisterous dogs. Or maybe he needed some quiet time and saw an opportunity to escape the chaos for a couple of minutes. Whatever, he told me that in about half an hour the soccer game in the park would end and the pathway would become a human-freeway for about fifteen minutes. I would get to witness the mayhem that they had to live with day in and day out. I knew this would be the perfect opportunity to show them how to handle the situation.

Immediately upon entering their home I was able to balance both Abby and Stella. Then I started to teach Bob and Janet the Game of Canine. I explained that the dogs were the only group scoring points here. The humans were getting annihilated. It was a shouting match.

"You must *Control the calm to win the game*. The only way to score points is to *get some calms*, which you guys are not doing because Abby and Stella are creating and controlling the chaos. Just as in the soccer game in the park behind your house, there are two opposing teams competing to win the game. The team with the most points is the winner. In the Game of Canine, whoever has the most points, by either controlling calms or creating excitement, wins the game."

At this point the soccer game ended. It was my chance to show Janet and Bob how balanced dogs behave.

As we headed out to their backyard I asked them both to remain on the porch, ensuring that their nervous energy would have no influence on Abby and Stella. I proceeded to the left side of the yard, adjacent to the pathway that was about to get crazy busy with people, dogs, bikes, skateboards, etc. I could hear and see families approaching so I stood directly in front of Abby and Stella, gave a light *pop* on each leash as I said, "Hey", with distinct authority. This proactive behavior on my part simply directed their attention to me. They both looked up and respectfully remained quiet. Abby gave a short halfhearted woof (it didn't qualify as a bark), resulting in my quietly repeating the 'Hey' sound. This was all that was required for Abby and Stella to remain calm, respectful and quiet for several minutes as dozens of people passed by.

As the crowd thinned out a little I asked Bob to come down and give it a try. Janet was in shock, with her hand over her mouth. She said, "I'm totally dumbfounded. Are these our dogs? I can't believe that they are so well-behaved and not going ballistic. Did you feed them something when we weren't looking?"

I smiled as Bob approached and I handed him the leash. I told him to repeat what I had done. He did this very well. Both dogs remained in their calm mode until the current group of passersby thinned out, so I asked Janet to give it a try. She declined and said she wanted to practice when even less people were around. Obviously, her nervousness was not what the dogs needed at this point, so I agreed.

I explained that the process was the same, at all three sides of the yard. It didn't matter if Sam was out next door, kids in the park were screaming after a goal or if it was rush-hour on the pathway. The humans had to take control, with green-ring leader-energy, to score all of the points and create a shutout of their own in the Game of Canine. In reality, all three of these scenarios could be taking place at the same time.

I gave Janet and Bob advice that would help them gain control of Abby and Stella from the back door versus continually having to leash them and stand in their face while next to a fence. I suggested that for several days they walk the perimeter of the yard with the dogs leashed, while keeping everyone calm, including themselves. "Progressively increase the distance that you stand away from them while they're still leashed before trying it without leashes." I stressed that they should not hurry with the process. "This will sound ridiculous, but the slower you go, the faster they will learn. Make each step 'solid' before moving on. By progressing too quickly, you will have to go back and redo things. Dog-time is slower than human-time."

Janet and Bob seemed to fully understand and were excited to practice the process. I also mentioned that Abby and Stella were in balance at this point, and that I would be leaving soon. It would then be their job to keep their dogs in this subservient, follower role by closely following the rules of the Game of Canine. I also cautioned that Abby and Stella were programmed to take back their dominant role and bark and protect their pack while in the yard, as this had been their previous habit. Both parties were on a mission of control. I said to Janet, "I bet you are a good cook and well versed in the art of following recipes."

She laughed and responded, "Bruce, I'll follow The Recipe to a 'T'."

"Who is going to be in control when I come back next week?" I asked. "What is the score of the Game of Canine going to be? How many points are the dogs going to score? What color will your ring be?"

They both smiled, nodding their heads up and down, totally understanding my point.

On my return visit the level of barking when I rang the doorbell was minimal. Bob and Janet took total control of the door. I was hugely impressed. Of course, the big challenge was going to happen in short order, as the soccer game in the park was about to end. We chatted about the process and how well things had progressed during the week.

They mentioned that their neighbour, Ray, had been blown away with the amount of control that they had gained in such a short time. He wanted me to drop over to evaluate his dog's aggressive behavior. It seems that his dog, Sam, had much worse things going on than just barking through the fence. She was horribly aggressive to all dogs. Their walks were hellish. I explained to Bob and Janet that I do my initial evaluation over the phone. If I stepped into Ray's house next door, it would be like one of the soccer players in the park stepping onto the soccer pitch. I would instantly be in-the-game and would have to deal with his dog. They understood, as they had witnessed firsthand how I immediately dealt with their dogs upon my arrival the previous week. I suggested that they ask Ray to give me a call so that we could talk about Sam.

At this point the soccer game ended, and it was game-on for Janet. Outside she went with both Westies, as Bob and I watched from the porch. Janet was very firm and proactive in managing the pair of them. Abby started to focus on the people passing by, but she didn't go off like an explosion as in the past. I was happy for Janet, and I could see Bob beaming with pride.

Janet and Bob didn't spend much time controlling the opposite side of the yard where Sam would normally stir up a commotion. Ray was very considerate and only allowed his dog out for short periods to give Bob and Janet lots of opportunity to be successful on the other two sides of their yard. This helped them tremendously. When Sam barked from her side of the fence, the barking triggered a primal response of territorial aggression, as the dogs perceived each other to be a pack-threatening enemy.

The following week I had a conversation with Ray regarding Sam's behavior. We set a day and time for me to come and balance Sam and teach Ray the *canine way*. Ray got incredible results with Sam after our first session, and their walks became pleasurable for them both. On my second visit, we all got together on the street to create a pack scenario with four dogs. I introduced Satchmo at this time for Ray and Sam's sake. Because of the close proximity of the dogs, I handled Sam while Ray handled Satchmo. Sam was a total lady while Satchmo, Abby and Stella all paraded past her on the sidewalk.

This new behavior was unprecedented. I was very pleased with Sam as she remained calm, cool and collected, despite the canine action within her grasp. Ray and I switched dogs. Sam only needed a couple of minor corrections from Ray to stay in a calm, non-aggressive mode. All in all, Ray was ecstatic with the results. He said to me, "My goal is to have the same control as you do when other dogs are present." He was confident that he would win the Game of Canine with Sam having zero points. I was impressed with both his confidence and determination.

Next, I suggested that everybody go into their respective backyards, so we could work on the barking through the fence. I went with Ray and Sam to watch from their side. Within only a few seconds and minimal correction from the humans, the dogs were sniffing face to face on opposite sides of the fence without any barking whatsoever, as all humans retained green-ring energy. Next, we all proceeded to the porch while the dogs wandered around their own yards, leash-free and without any fuss at the fence line. No negative energy. It was hard to believe this was brand new behavior because it appeared to be natural to all three canines.

"Isn't it awesome to have balanced dogs?"

## **Summary**

One of the basic rules to the Game of Canine is; *Control the door.* In the case of front-doors and yard perimeters, the same holds true. Although the front-door area has limited space and the yard is much greater, the game is identical. If a dog is in the yard and someone approaches, he will feel the need to bark and protect his territory. A couple of barks are a warning to both their owner and whoever is approaching. Any more barking qualifies as points being scored by the dog. If your dog barks and you calm him quickly, then it is you who scores.

I know that when Satchmo barks while in the yard (usually only once or twice), he is letting me know that something is amiss. He sits at the back door until I arrive to let him in or I go outside to see who is in the driveway. This is Satchmo showing respect, so I score a point.

When a dog barks at the door or fence, the question to ask yourself is; Which side of the door/fence is your dog barking at? If the cadence of his barks is short, rapid and continuous, he is likely barking at the other side of the door/fence. Often, a short rapid bark is a result of insecurity. He is saying, "My pack is here. Stay away." The continuous barking is to make him appear formidable.

I believe the more noise dogs make, the more insecure they are. On the other hand, when a dog barks only a couple of times he is warning his leader of danger, as well as whoever is on the other side of the door/fence. This bark could be accompanied with a low, steady warning growl.

My next-door neighbour has a small, yappy Cavalier King Charles Spaniel. When in the yard he barks endlessly. When I have had enough of his racket I let Satchmo out into the yard. Immediately the Spaniel's barking stops, and he comes over to meet Satchmo, who is calmly sniffing through the fence. Satchmo's calm, strong energy mitigates the barking of the neighbour's dog. Before he walks away, Satchmo lifts his leg and pees on the fence, to get in the last word of posturing.

## Chapter 26

## Soiling

*Marking is not an accident.*

I was a little shocked at the inordinate amount of dog poop that needed to be cleaned up one wet, rainy morning. It is totally irresponsible for dog owners to not pick up after their dog. I understand that a dog can run all around the park and not be noticed by his owner 100 percent of the time. Therefore, sometimes when dogs poop, it may unintentionally not be picked up. That is partially why I volunteer, and I truly enjoy my time at the dog park, meeting both dogs and owners on Sunday mornings. If people didn't help with the maintenance at the park it would soon become a cesspool and unusable, instead of a beautiful and clean environment for dogs to run free. In theory, if each dog owner did their job of picking up after their dog, my volunteer job would almost be redundant.

On many occasions I've seen owners watch their dog defecate at the park and then knowingly ignore the event and walk away, as if they were in the middle of a forest. I watched as it just happened again. I approached the owner to hand him a poop bag and reminded him, as the sign at the park entrance indicates, that it was his job to clean up after his dog. I also mentioned that I was a volunteer, along with the fact that we are short of helpers. I then asked him if he would like to sign up for some volunteer hours.

The typical response is, "Ah, um, no . . . I'm sorry but I'm too busy", as they walk away.

Shortly after this incident, a stout man wearing well-worn pants, a dress shirt and running shoes, came over to me and asked if I was Brewster. I smiled, nodded and offered him my hand. As we shook hands he told me his name was Harry and asked if I knew anything about housebreaking a dog. I didn't think he was referring to the medium-sized black Border Collie that he had with him, named Mindy. She was certainly not a puppy. In fact, I would have guessed her to be about four or five years old. It turned out that he was indeed talking about Mindy. I asked him Mindy's age and was surprised when he told me that she was six years old – and still not housebroken!

My first thought was that Harry's house must smell awful after six years of indoor soiling.

I asked him if Mindy did her business in one area of the home, maybe a mud room or basement.

"She tends to go in the kitchen", he said.

I was flabbergasted that this man, who appeared intelligent and professional, would tolerate this behavior from Mindy for so long. I asked if she used pee-pads and he told me that she had when she was a puppy. I was taken aback as I imagined a dog peeing and pooping in *my* kitchen for six years. Harry's kitchen floor must be discolored and smell like a urinal, not to mention the issue of hygiene in the room where food is prepared.

I knew Harry needed some serious help. I said to him, "The good news is that both you and Mindy are smart individuals, so the solution should be a no brainer." He smiled slightly and then told me about Mindy being quick to learn tricks, along with her learning from a very early age not to enter his home office, where he worked as a stockbroker. He added that she was moderately obedience trained with minimal effort from Harry. I asked if he used treats as part of his positive reinforcement while teaching Mindy various commands. He said that Mindy's favorite treat was a carrot.

It was my turn to smile as I knew it would be a cinch to get a bright dog like Mindy to use the outdoors for her washroom. Again, I wondered why an intelligent man with a smart dog would tolerate this negative behavior for such a length of time. I asked Harry if he lived alone with Mindy. He told me that he's been a widower for the past six years. His wife, Liz, had bought the puppy for him when she was diagnosed with a terminal disease. She felt that Harry would need some company because he was somewhat of an introvert and needed a reason to get out of the house. He also explained that his energy level and his mental state were both at an all-time low when Liz past away, and that his depression had lasted for several years.

Suddenly things became clear to me as to why Harry hadn't put in the effort and time to housebreak his best friend. It was easier not to deal with it. At this point Harry's eyes were tearing up. He continued to talk about how wonderful his life had been before Liz passed and how fortunate he was to have had her as his life partner for so many wonderful years. The energy at this point of our conversation was very low. I needed to brighten things up, so I asked if they had any previous dogs. He told me about Carlos, a rescue German Shepherd mix. He had been very well trained as both Liz and Harry had gone to obedience classes when Carlos was very young. He was their pride and joy. They didn't have any children and the dog had passed away more than twenty years before.

I asked Harry how he knew my name. He mentioned his nephew Jessie had a buddy whose family had used my services. They'd ask me to help save their family Dogo Argentino, named Emmitt, from being put down because of his major aggression. I remembered Emmitt. How could I forget him? Harry reminded me that Emmitt was 180 pounds of being either extremely friendly or extremely aggressive. The question was always what would you receive from Emmitt, a sloppy lick or a nasty bite? His turnaround was successful and very rewarding, as a super-friendly yet slobbering mass of white fur was saved from the needle.

Harry's mood seemed to brighten, so I knew now was the time to give him some pointers on housebreaking Mindy. I indicated that this was a process predicated on positive reinforcement, with verbal praise accompanied by petting and treating her with some carrots. I said, "There is no such thing as too much praise when building positive results. If she soils in the house more than ten seconds before your discovering it, then ignore it and calmly clean it up." I explained that a dog's short-term memory is only about ten seconds. "If you discipline her after ten seconds she will not know what you are giving her heck for. If you catch her in the act, then interrupt her with a clap and/or a 'Hey' sound. Then calmly, yet firmly, escort her outside with the hope that she will finish what she started inside."

"When she does any business outdoors," I said, "give her huge praise, a rub and then a carrot or her favorite ball or toy. Always give the rubbing praise first, before the treat. This gives her two forms of love, which is better than only one. If you don't have a treat with you, an excited rub will suffice as she will recognize this as the primary form of praise/love from you." I asked him if he had ever seen a police drug-sniffing dog find drugs on TV. The handler pulls out the dog's favorite chew toy or ball. The drug discovery is like a game, and the reward is a huge injection of praise and exuberance by the handler. "You don't have to make as big a deal as that, but you get the idea."

"Dogs are creatures of habit, just like humans. This makes it much easier to predict when Mindy will likely need to relieve herself. When we get up in the morning, the first thing we tend to do is use the bathroom. Canines are very similar. Use the mornings as the most predictable time that she will need to relieve herself. After only a few mornings of outdoor peeing, along with giving huge hugs and carrots, Mindy will very quickly be waiting for you to come downstairs to take her out. She is very bright, and this consistent timing will trigger her new behavior."

The next trick was for Harry to predict other times when Mindy needed to relieve herself. For example, about twenty minutes after eating in the morning she would likely need to poop. Harry then told me that he took his shower while Mindy was eating her breakfast. I mentioned that time management in housebreaking is crucial. I suggested that he make a necessary adjustment and shower before he fed her. He would then be able to give her the attention required to be successful by taking her outside about twenty minutes after eating and repeat the positive reinforcement routine when she needs to eliminate.

I continued, “Your consistent actions will create a routine for Mindy to get used to. By taking her out more often than usual throughout the day, you will be able to provide her with extra opportunities to make use of the backyard versus the kitchen floor. I know that if you are true to making the small effort needed to facilitate the new routine, she will get with the program in no time. Eventually, and within a shorter period than you may think, she will be using the yard versus the kitchen for her bathroom duties. Remember there is no such thing as too much positive reinforcement when she does what you want. This will build a positive association, which encourages her to repeat the behavior.”

Harry fully understood the lesson and had only one question. “How often during the day should I take her outside?”

“Lots, even when you don’t think she needs to go. She may just have a short pee.” I also suggested that he walk Mindy several times per day; morning, midday and evening would be ideal. I indicated that she must walk respectfully beside him and not pulling in front.

“This will build her respect and trust while she remains subordinate to you. It will also solidify your pack ranking, to be superior to her, and will eradicate any of her soiling being a result of marking. In the wild, only leader’s mark their territory.” Harry whined a little about his bad knee, that made long walks very difficult. I asked him if he could handle a five-minute walk, two-and-a half-minutes in each direction.

“Sure”, he said with a smile.

“That’s all you need if she walks respectfully in a heel position beside you.” I said. “This doesn’t replace other forms of exercise. She still needs to burn off energy.”

Harry said that a five minute walk would be perfect. He could walk down his laneway and back: once to get the newspaper in the morning; around midday to pick up his mail; and late in the afternoon to check for any deliveries. Seems, he was an Amazon junkie and was always ordering things online.

He was smiling and playful with Mindy as he repeated the process back to me. His demeanour was significantly more cheerful. It is not often that someone is so thorough when repeating what they just learned. Again, I smiled. My earlier guess of his intelligence was clearly confirmed. Mindy was in for a huge change in her life and certainly for the better. My guess; Harry would soon replace his kitchen floor.

**Dog Whisperer Story; a couple of pee-obsessed low-riders**

Molly, a retired schoolteacher, was downsizing from a large country home to a city townhouse. Her anguish was caused by her two Dachshunds, Bogey and Birdie, who soiled or marked in her farmhouse regularly, ruining almost all the original century-old hardwood floors. I assumed, given the dogs' names, that Molly was an avid golfer.

She mentioned that she'd been referred to me by her new vet. Her move-in date was just over a couple of weeks away as her new townhouse was undergoing renovations.

"I am having beautiful, new hardwood floors installed throughout my new home as we speak", she said. "I am sick about the idea that the dogs will ruin them with their peeing." She then asked if it was possible to stop her dogs from peeing in the new house? Marking is common, and fortunately, easy to cure. I was encouraging and said I could meet with her before she was to move and assured her it would be enough time to balance her dogs and teach her how to take control, via the Game of Canine.

"Once you are in the driver's seat, and Bogey and Birdie move to the backseat, then the problem should dissipate immediately", I said. She was doubtful.

We met at her new townhouse, which was under attack by an army of workmen scurrying about trying to make their deadline. When I arrived both dogs were barking feverishly. My guess is that they were both in a state of panic, due to the number of workers coming and going, hammers banging, and the intense sound of power tools. It seemed I'd arrived at an ideal time because the workers were all outside on a coffee break. Once I balanced Bogey and Birdie, we headed to the kitchen because it was the only room not being worked on.

I mentioned to Molly that if Bogey and Birdie came to my home for a sleepover, they would not likely pee in my house and would only use the outdoors to do their business.

"How would they know not to pee in your house?" she asked.

"The answer is pack balance. It's the key to unleashing a dog's true potential. Bogey and Birdie viewed me as their new leader and the new pack hierarchy would not change if they lived with me. It is the leader's job to mark his territory and not the follower's."

I went on to explain the importance of who leaves their mark in a wolf pack. The leader is the only male to lift his leg to mark his territory. All the other male pack members must squat. The reason is to mark higher on a tree or pole to make themselves appear bigger to any roaming wolves. Domestic male dogs typically (but not all) lift their leg to pee to appear bigger as well.

"If both dogs remain in the follower role, as they currently are, it is not a follower's job to mark their territory, and therefore the peeing should stop." I couldn't resist joking: "It's now your job to pee in the corner." It worked. We both laughed. It was now *my* job to teach Molly how to keep Bogey and Birdie in a balanced follower role, while realigning her position as the new alpha/leader of her pack. I told Molly to closely follow The Recipe and the results would be dramatic and immediate.

When I returned the next week, I was met in the driveway by Molly, Bogey and Birdie. The house was still full of workers completing the final touches in the home. We sat in her backyard at the picnic table and had a glass of iced tea as we chatted for about twenty minutes. Molly was brimming with pride and excitement. She couldn't wait to start the conversation. I didn't need to ask her how things were going. It was written all over her smiling face.

"They haven't peed once in the house since you left", she said. "I followed the rules diligently and I'm at the top of my game now; it's like I'm playing *par* golf, which by the way, I have never done."

"My friends and daughter can't believe that Bogey and Birdie have not wrecked my new floors. Not once in a week . . . but Bogie did at my daughter's house one day when she was dog sitting while I was out shopping for new drapes. She has a beautiful Barbet dog named Pierre who constantly bullies Bogey."

I suggested that Bogey was marking to rank with Pierre. I reiterated that ranking was the foremost thought on a dog's mind.

"They don't seem nearly as edgy", she said, "and their barking has reduced to a totally acceptable level. I can calm them within five seconds without any problem, which means I score the points and not them. A week ago, they would have been barking and totally upset with all the workers in the house. Now it's not an issue. Isn't that amazing?"

I laughed and gave her huge congratulations, because the positive results were life-changing for them all; Bogey, Birdie and Molly. The dogs were much happier being subservient to her and not being forced to take the alpha role, while Molly got to enjoy a pee-free new home. A happy time was had by all, including me as I enjoyed the glee in Molly's voice and smile. She gave me a big hug of thanks as I was leaving. She then added that her daughter would be giving me a call about Pierre.

**Summary**

Soiling (peeing and pooping) in the house is commonly predicated on a dog having a dominant mindset. Dogs believe that it is their job to mark their territory. Sometimes the dog has simply not been housetrained and taught to do his business outside. Perhaps the dog has a health issue, or is so excited he can't control himself. Sometimes there's an accident because of human error – he wasn't let outside in time.

In the above two examples, Harry's and Molly's problems were cured by their taking charge and controlling the situation. In Harry's case he hadn't taken responsibility for teaching Mindy to go outside. He was lax, due to his depression. With Molly, she was not perceived by Bogey and Birdie to be their leader, and they were also allowed to get away with their indoor peeing.

By being strong leaders and establishing a timely routine for outdoor bathroom habits, dogs will naturally learn, and very quickly I might add, to do their eliminating outdoors. They *want* to go outside as it is natural for them. Dogs don't like to eliminate in their living space. Timing is everything with this process, especially with puppies. Try to be consistent. Let them out early in the morning, shortly after all meals and frequently between meals, at least one time throughout the evening, and of course before bed.

To teach a young puppy this process, it will help if you use a crate for sleeping and, upon getting up in the morning, immediately take the pup outside. Remember; give huge praise and rewards when the trip outdoors is a success. Often people will buy a crate that is far too big, like a condo, which provides enough space for the dog to soil away from their bed area. I suggest a crate big enough for them to be able to easily stand, turn around and lie down in, but not too much bigger. Often crates have an adjustable wall within the crate to facilitate growth of the puppy. This way a larger crate can start out small and increase in size as needed, so you don't need to buy multiple sizes of crates.

## Chapter 27

## Insecurity; *Nervous Nellie*

*Strong leadership will inspire confidence.*

On a brutally cold December morning, nearing noon, I was thinking about having a hot bowl of soup for lunch. I normally only hang around the dog park until midday, because I can easily get my list of jobs completed by then. I was chilled to the bone and wishing I had a remote start in my car, so I could fire up the engine and in about 10 minutes hop into a cozy warm vehicle and go home.

My thoughts were interrupted by a lady who was fast approaching with a determined look on her face. Trotting along with her was her Shetland Sheepdog. I thought this was a good day for a long-haired Sheltie to keep warm. It made me realize just how cold I was, and the thought flashed through my mind that I wished I'd left ten minutes early. Then I changed my mind. I could tell by the look on her face that she had a serious dog problem. I revel passing on my knowledge to people and helping families/packs become balanced. It's tremendously rewarding, a feel-good-all-over sensation that I get to experience on a regular basis. My eyes often well up when I work with people and their dogs. I guess I'm a softie . . . and proud of it.

"Good morning. Are you Brewster, the dog guy?" she called as she swiftly approached and shook my hand with a noticeably firm grip. I had the feeling that this woman was on an urgent mission. She introduced herself as Edna and told me her dog's name was Lady. I dug into my memory bank and tried to recall seeing Lady on previous days.

I did recall seeing her, always wandering near the fence with no other dogs nearby, sticking close to Edna. She would sniff around but not run free. After all, this was a leash-free park where dogs get to kick up their heels and let off some steam, but not Lady.

Edna mentioned that a couple who lived in her neighbourhood had used my services with magical results. I distinctly remembered the couple, whose fearful, nervous Norfolk Terrier had deeply touched my heart. It would be difficult to forget such a nervous dog. Tessa lived behind the couch, and her owners had never touched her or picked her up since rescuing her about three weeks before. She immediately came out of her shell when I entered the home. She looked at me with her soft, sensitive eyes as if to say, "I'm so glad that you are here. I feel better already. These nice folks are confusing me and not making me feel protected. In fact, they keep sending me the message that they want me to lead and protect them. I'm so nervous I can't come out from behind the couch, where I feel somewhat safe." This case ended beautifully as the little terrier instantly gained confidence as soon as she was balanced.

Edna went on to tell me about Lady and her problems. "Lady has a plethora of insecurities and odd behaviors", she said, "including soiling in the house, both peeing and pooping. She won't go outside through the back door, only the front door. She won't go upstairs or downstairs and therefore, lives on the main floor only. She doesn't like any loud noises, thunder, my dropping anything on the floor, or slamming of doors. She walks down the street with panic in her eyes.

All in all, she is an extremely skittish and nervous dog. Is there anything that you can do to help her?"

My heart was heavy. Life for Lady was a constant struggle. Her feelings of insecurity, panic and worry must have been taking years off her life. I bet her blood pressure was off the chart. I asked if Lady barked at all noises or situations. Edna indicated that she barked at every noise outside and she went nuts when the landscapers arrive to either cut the grass or shovel the snow. "This happens often as I live alone on a two-acre property on the waterfront. I need the place looked after. Workers are on my property at least a couple of times a week. When they arrive, Lady sits on my lap. She shakes or vibrates the whole time."

I told Edna that I felt Lady's problems were totally fixable but not from where we are standing. It was going to be a much bigger job than what I could accomplish standing in the middle of a park, on a very cold winter day. By this time Lady was calmly lying between us, displaying no nervousness or insecurity whatsoever. I also mentioned that Lady seemed fine now and that she was the only one of us that seemed to be warm. "Do you have any idea why she is so relaxed?"

Edna nodded her head and then said, "My friends told me that you have magical energy and changed their dog's life within a few minutes."

"Edna, I don't do magic", I said. "Yes, I do have calm, strong energy, but so do lots of people, just as you can. There is no magic in what I teach. Knowledge is power, and my pleasure comes from sharing my knowledge. Your friends and their dog became a balanced pack. The key to unleashing their dog's insecurity was that they implicitly followed The Recipe, or the rules to the Game of Canine."

By now I was the one shaking, due to the cold wind. I pondered for a moment, wondering if there was anything that I could tell her to give her and Lady some immediate relief. The only thing that came to mind was that this case had no short answers and that I needed to be in their house and work with them both. I mentioned this to Edna, who was more than willing to set up a time for me to come to her home. We decided on the following Wednesday morning.

Satchmo was running around trying to keep warm, so I whistled for him to come as we all headed to our vehicles. I can't recall ever being so happy to get out of the wind and into my car. Even if it was freezing inside the car, I was out of the wind and I knew that it would only be a few minutes until the heater was doing its job and melting the ice off my beard.

On Wednesday I arrived at Edna's rather palatial home and was greeted by the sound of Lady's rapid, nervous bark. As soon as the door opened, I handed Edna a slip lead to put on Lady, who was standing in front of Edna, barking nonstop. By the time Edna handed the leash back to me, Lady had stopped barking and was calmly standing next to me. Suddenly Lady seemed much less stressed. At that point I said, "Balance is natural for dogs. It's in canine DNA. She knows that the leader's job is now clearly filled and that she is not obligated in any way to act in a dominant, protective manner. This new realignment of the pecking order finally releases Lady to enjoy the relaxing mindset of a follower."

As we stood in Edna's cavernous, stone-floored front hallway, which had winding stairs heading up to the second floor, I asked, "Are these the stairs that she won't climb?" Edna nodded. I then asked her to stay where she was standing and to please remain quiet. I started up the stairs with Lady in tow and made my way up to the landing. I turned around to partially descend the staircase before I did an about-face and headed back upwards before making a final change in direction down to the front hall. Miss Lady was about one step behind me the whole time. In fact, she didn't miss a beat throughout the whole process.

I next asked Edna to show me the back door that Lady had issues going through. Once we arrived in the kitchen she started telling me how Lady would normally start getting nervous as they approached the kitchen table on their way to the back door. I reiterated to Edna to please not talk and just let Lady process things on her own without influence. I purposely fiddled with the lock for about five seconds before I opened it. Lady only hesitated for a brief second as I headed outside. No negative behavior whatsoever. Once outside, I turned to come back, Lady hesitated, and the leash became tight. I stopped, turned toward Lady and waited with the leash snug but not tight. This sent a message to Lady that I wanted her to follow me, but that I was OK for her to process this in her time, not mine.

Edna, once again, started to say something, but I caught her as I put my hand up, at which time Lady started through the door. We repeated this in-and-out process several more times with no hesitation on Lady's part. Next, I handed Edna the leash and asked her to lead Lady in and out of the door several times and then up and down the stairs. At that point both of us had tears of joy in our eyes. Lady had been released of her mental restraints.

Here's a quick review of what happened, from Lady's point of view. Before I rang the doorbell, she sensed me. Even though she barked rapidly, expressing her nervousness (which was her habit), she went into the role of protector because Edna was not filling the leader's position. I call this a *double negative,* e.g., when a nervous, insecure dog (the first negative) is forced to take on the leader's role and protect her pack (the second negative). Lady was also positioned in front of Edna, which physically put her in the driver's seat and Edna in the backseat (or the position of follower).

As soon as the door opened, Lady commenced her progression to the follower's position, all with no resistance on her part. It was simply the Superman-like ability of canines to read energy and react to my calm leader-energy. It is typical for humans to under appreciate the canine's ability to sense energy, their No. 1 way to communicate, whether it is around corners or through doors. Dogs are *supersonic* at this. We must learn to appreciate and respect this powerful ability. Lady instantly knew that I presented no aggression or fear, only green-ring energy.

After I taught Edna the rules to the Game of Canine, we went for a walk and Edna took the leash. Lady walked just like the refined lady she is. No fear, no pulling or any other negative actions. All was good. I was beaming with sheer pleasure as I witnessed the transformation of this pack. As Edna practised what she had learned, the pack remained in good balance with Lady contentedly accepting the follower role. No longer was she obligated to protect Edna when workmen were on site, at the door or making noises outside. She became rather oblivious to the whole scene. As Edna's leadership skills developed, along with her green-ring energy (void of pity), she proficiently climbed her Leader Ladder. Magical – yes. Magic – not a chance.

Edna came to the leash-free park a couple of Sundays later. What a difference; Lady wandered away from Edna as soon as they entered the gate. I headed over to Edna to congratulate her on Lady's carefree demeanour. As we were discussing Lady's phenomenal progress she gleefully pointed and said, "She is playing with the Manchester Terrier." I said, "Boy that tickles my heart. That's Stein. He was previously stricken with extreme separation anxiety."

I asked her about Lady's soiling and insecurity. She said, "Bruce, it's unbelievable. She hasn't peed or pooped in the house once since your visit. She hardly barks at the workmen anymore, and on her walks, she confidently holds her head up like she's royalty." I asked Edna if she could explain why the soiling instantly stopped. She smiled knowingly and said, "The key to unlocking Lady's angst was pack balance. Lady went from the confused mindset of going in and out of the leader's position to knowing that I was clearly in charge. Therefore, she was happily relegated to follower, and followers don't mark their territory nor act as protectors."

I was totally impressed and gave her two thumbs up, along with a big hug. I said, "Wow, you got it, girl."

Edna added, “Bruce, if your Recipe was for baking a cake, you’d have an award-winning creation.”

**Dog Whisperer Story; Standard Poodle's mental breakdown**

A couple in a neighbouring city, Jody and Tracey, got in touch with me regarding Maple, their four-year-old Standard Poodle. Maple was a rescue dog that was found wandering alone in a huge city park. She was believed to be a puppy-mill dog, which would typically have eight litters in her four-year tenure as a breeding bitch. I can't imagine how a person kicks a dog out on their own, knowing that she would not likely survive. Pathetic as it is, I guess that's part of their plan. In High Park, where she was found, packs of coyotes would have made dinner of her.

A puppy-mill bitch typically lives in a crate almost her entire life. Her sole purpose is to reproduce to her maximum capacity with only one goal; to make money for her owners. Health concerns for the dogs are minimal, if any. Mass production is priority No. 1. They are usually sold to agents who have connections with privately owned pet stores, as the big franchises tend not to sell dogs. Frogs maybe, but not dogs. A puppy-mill dog can sell for as much as purebred dogs from breeders. When viewed through the glass cage in a pet store, they're irresistible, especially to children.

Several years ago, I was putting in some time while waiting for a friend in a mall. As I wandered around I ended up in a pet store. Like all patrons, I was drawn to the windows displaying the puppies. There were several different mixed breeds and they all looked infectiously cute. There is no such thing as an ugly puppy. The prices were handwritten on the glass of each cage and varied from $700 to $2,300.

I was blown away by how expensive they were, knowing that a quality breeder would likely charge less. A puppy from a breeder would likely have minimal health issues, come with a written health guarantee, along with the pedigree. The difference in the two options (a dog from a quality breeder versus a puppy-mill dog) was irrelevant to these children. The only thing that mattered was which dog was the cutest and could they *please, please, please* take one home? As I looked over the heads of several children, who had their noses pinned to the glass while giggling and pointing to each pup in the cage, I was asked by their father, "How do you choose just one?"

I looked him in the eye and said rather quietly, "You should not buy a dog in a pet store. Always get a dog from an accredited breeder or rescue group. These dogs are from a puppy mill. Go home and get on the internet and find the breed and breeder that fits your needs." He looked bewildered, like a deer in the headlights, so I repeated myself and said, "Do not buy a dog from a pet store. Take your kids out of here." I immediately walked out of the store. I knew I wouldn't be very popular with the owner, if he'd overheard what I said.

When I spoke to Tracey on the phone, she told me that Maple was totally withdrawn, rarely left her bed and would not have anything to do with her husband, Jody, or their adult son, John. "What can we do for her?" she asked with desperation in her voice. Her concern for Maple was painfully evident. I immediately wanted to help. She also mentioned that cost was not an issue. She said, "We have the means, if you have the skill to help our girl." I guess at that point I could have doubled my fees, but of course I charge everyone the same rate, relative to the breed and severity of issues. In other words, the fee for a vicious, biting 150-pound power breed would be dramatically different from, say the fee for Maple, a 45-pound withdrawn, insecure poodle.

When I arrived at their home all was silent. Not a creature was stirring, especially not Maple. Normally a dog wants to see who is visiting. If I hadn't known any better, even after I was in the home and introduced to everyone, I would never have guessed they had a dog. We went into the living room and all was revealed. Beside the sofa there was an oval dog bed. Maple was all curled up and not even looking our way. It looked like she wanted to pull the covers up over her head. I had never witnessed such insecurity and mental anguish in a dog. The word 'withdrawn' would be a gross understatement. I had to take a few deep breaths while pondering my next move. I was asking myself how I could give this frightened little girl some of my strength.

I asked the family to sit down and not talk as I sat opposite them on the couch, beside her bed. I kept taking slow deep breaths. As I sensed my own anxiety, I knew that Maple could read me better than anyone in the room. I needed to connect with her, not the humans at this point. It was imperative to give her the message that she needed the most: "I'm here to help you and not hurt you. I'm calm, I'm strong, and I am the new leader of the pack."

My eyes filled with tears. *I* was absorbing *her* energy, not the other way around. I tried to logically calculate if my emotion was good or bad from Maple's point of view. I decided that whatever I was feeling was natural and I didn't try to control myself. Finally, I started to feel my strength return and I knew that Maple was feeling all the emotion I was giving off. All this time she had not moved a muscle. She stayed in her curled-up position, her back toward me, never once lifting her head to look up. It was like she was asleep. She was overcome by insecurity and fear.

As I look back and analyze my rollercoaster ride of emotions, I realize that by showing compassion and softness, she felt my softer side. Also, with hindsight, I understand why she related better to Tracey versus Jody and John. It was because of her mothering and nurturing softness. I know I am a confident and rather strong person, but I also have a real soft side. That said, I had never been overcome with such emotion from any dog. I decided that I would leave Maple as she lay. My *modus operandi* has always been to first leash a dog, balance him, move him around a little and then have him stay beside me as I teach my lessons. Maple broke the mold and I was flying by the seat-of-my-pants at this point. I didn't know how I was going to proceed with her at first. I had no plan, I just knew that I should listen to my intuition. I learned a very long time ago that our intuition is never wrong.

The level of Maple's insecurity was discussed in detail as the family and I talked. She lived in her bed for almost every twenty-four-hour period. Tracey would bring food and water to the side the bed, so she could eat and drink. Maple never went for walks and would not engage in any play other than sitting on Tracey's lap, while shaking most of the time.

If either of the men approached, she would shake in fear. If they lifted her onto their lap, the stress would cause her to pee. This was painful for them to witness. The only time that she left her bed was to go outside to do her business. At that point I asked Tracey to take Maple outside. She proceeded to pick her up and started for the kitchen door. I said, "Whoa, what are you doing?"

She answered, "You said to take her outside, so that's what I'm doing."

"Can't she walk? Do you have to carry her?" I asked.

Tracey told me that Maple was able to walk but that she had always carried her outside. When she put her down outside, Maple did her business within a very short radius of where she was put down. She didn't sniff or wander around the yard. She simply stood still until Tracey carried her back into the house. I was blown away how deep Maple had withdrawn into her mental shell. I asked Tracey to put Maple back into her bed. I looked over at her and again I sensed that she just wanted to pull the covers up over her head and bury herself away from the rest of the world, under the covers.

After I completed teaching the family the Game of Canine, it was time to interact with Miss Scaredy-Pants. I had been there for about two hours and Maple had not moved other than when Tracey temporarily picked her up. I reached down to give her a couple of gentle reassuring rubs and then slipped my leash on her. I gave the leash a soft tug but got no results. I gave a firmer pull and she came to life. She stood up and stepped out of her bed. The family started to comment on her new activity, so I quickly put my finger to my lips indicating for them not to talk. I continued with a slight pressure on the leash, and to my joy Maple started to walk toward me. I moved into the dining room and she nervously followed. Next, I went through the kitchen, into the front hallway and finally completed my circle back into the living room. I reached down and gave Maple some pats of praise and, as usual, said nothing.

Next, I suggested to the family that we all go outside. All three of them quietly raised their eyebrows with a look of surprise on their face. I headed to the door with Maple in tow. She walked tentatively with her tail tucked under, but she didn't resist.

Once outside I asked the family to wait in the driveway as Maple and I headed up the street. The idea here was to get out of their energy zone for Maple's sake. This eliminated any pity, nervousness or apprehension on their part. It was now just the two of us. I looked down and her tail was now straight out parallel to the ground, indicating calmness, free of fear. This was absolutely a revelation, to say the least. By the time we were about two houses away, her tail was straight up and she was actually prancing like a Standard Poodle. At this point I was about to cry but I kept things in check for her sake. If she could talk, Maple would have been singing. She had a smile on her snout, her eyes were sparkling, and she had a snap in her step. This was a new dog, never to return to her old self. I was over the top with joy.

We walked back to the driveway and I handed the leash to Tracey, who had her hand over her mouth in astonishment. I said, "Don't talk or question it. Just start to walk." Maple instantly followed her up the street with the same vigou and joy. It is a picture that I still have in my mind; one of those classics that never fades.

Now for the best part: As Tracey and Maple returned, I asked Jody to give it a try and off they went with the same results. John repeated the process for Maple's fourth jaunt up the street. John even ran with her. She galloped and leaped with glee. As we stood and chatted about the miraculous event that we had all just experienced, Maple sniffed and snooped around the front yard while John kept moving to keep up with her. This was certainly a welcome change of events.

While we watched the new Maple adventuring around the yard, I mentioned all the new scents that she must be experiencing. She hadn't used her nose in a curious way since they rescued her, about four months prior. Her nose was her No. 1 sense. Dogs are born with the ability to smell but without vision or hearing. For her to not use her nose told me how lost she was. To start using it after all this time is sensational.

We weren't very talkative as we were all focused on the 45-pound bone-rack of a dog wandering about the front lawn, experiencing life as she had never before. Maple had lived in a cage most of her life and was then tossed into the wilderness to survive on her own. Fortunately, someone found her and took her to an animal shelter, where she was again put into a cage. The final leg of her journey was being rescued by some very special people when she was so low she was living in a *mental prison*. Maple had just won the lottery of life.

Jody finally spoke: "We have a new dog, I can't believe it." His eyes were lit up with joy.

"If we are all in awe watching this take place", I said, "can you imagine how spectacular Miss Maple feels? The good news is that she doesn't think about the past, like humans, she only lives in the moment. All of her past hardships are over."

Maple had remained in her depressed state because Jody, Tracey and John all felt so very sorry for her. Their sadness and sorrow were the very energy that told Maple that they were all weak. From Maple's viewpoint, if they weren't leaders, then the job was forced onto her. She was fragile in the first place, and all this added pressure to lead the pack resulted in a dog that had a mental breakdown and completely withdrew into herself: the *double negative*.

I am a very compassionate person when it comes to humans. But I also know that if one shows pity, it indicates weakness to dogs. From a human point of view, I sometimes appear somewhat insensitive. But I am expressing strength from a dog's perspective. I don't worry what humans think because it is the canine that I need to impress. My guess is that Maple was abused by men in the breeding period of her life. These men would not be compassionate, only impersonal and indifferent. She sensed my softer side, along with my strength, and *reacted* to the situation. She did not use logic or analysis like humans do. Dogs simply react. No one else would have expected such a miraculous turnaround in such short order. Pack balance is not to be underestimated. It is what freed Maple from her depression.

A couple of months after my sessions with Maple and her pack, I was visiting a local doggie-day-care that I'd recommended to Jody and Tracey. Karen, one of the owners, mentioned that Maple was now a regular guest and that she happened to be there on this day. Tracey had informed them about Maple's history and how she was now a new dog. I asked Karen about Maple's behavior. I wondered where Maple positioned herself within the pack of other day-care guests. Karen informed me that she was not at the top of the pecking order, nor at the bottom, but somewhere in the middle. It was enlightening to hear that Maple positioned herself above some other dogs. This meant that she was getting even stronger and more confident. Music to my ears.

**Summary**

When dealing with insecure dogs beware of the *double negative* factor. The first negative is that they are *Nervous Nellies.* The second negative is forcing an insecure dog to take on the role of the leader. This is like forcing a young, insecure child, with low self-esteem, to protect their mother and father from bad guys. It is supposed to be the parents who make a child feel safe and protected, not vice-versa.

The best tack with a timid, insecure dog is to give them strength and confidence through your green-ring energy, because they'll sense this. If, however, you are angry, upset, inconsistent, nervous, afraid, sorrowful or show pity, they will perceive that you are weak, therefore you are not going to protect or lead them. By the law of canine nature, the absence of a leader forces them to take on the leader's job. Remember: Never get upset, raise your voice or make them feel threatened in any way. Also, don't baby and coddle them by giving in to them when they don't want to do something. A dog cannot be treated like a child and a child cannot be treated like a dog.

When I met Lady and Maple, in the above stories, I gave them strength through my calm, strong, green-ring energy. Dogs innately know exactly what our energy says. I was not a threat of any kind, nor did I show pity toward them, because this is not what canines feel. I had compassion for them but didn't take *no* for an answer. I also let them do things on dog-time.

If we rescue a dog, we tend to grieve with a heavy heart because of their negative past. But this is human behavior, not canine behavior. Even if they were abused, hurt in the past or are blind with only three legs, dogs don't feel sorry for each other. In a wild canine pack, dogs nurture each other by bringing food to injured pack mates who can't hunt for themselves or to a bitch watching over her young brood. They are pack animals and put the pack before themselves, not without some emotion, but nowhere near to what we feel. The emotion that humans express requires the ability to reason and evaluate.

Canines live in the moment, so the past is the past. They have a very short memory bank but a long-term association. If a rescue dog had previously been hit with a broom and you brought out the broom, he is likely to negatively associate the presence of the broom. This negative response can easily be reversed so that the broom becomes a positive association. This would likely be a slow process where the broom would be presented from a distance. When the dog remained calm while it was in view be sure to give lots of praise and positive reinforcement. Very slowly, over many days or weeks if need be, decrease the distance between the dog and the broom, adding praise, treats and positive reinforcement if she remains calm.

I suggest that this should be a quiet process; don't talk and you will be far more effective. Although, it's *easier* said than *done*. The goal would be that the dog doesn't feel threatened by the broom. The end game would be for the dog to be near the broom with no apprehension. The timing for such a goal should always be on dog-time; not fast paced human-time. If you move forward too quickly, because of impatience, you will end up taking many steps backward.

# Chapter 28

## Crates, Kennels and Vets

*Crates are a dog's personal den.*

A young boy approached me one day while I was taking a break from my duties at the dog park. I had my eyes closed and was meditating under the big shade tree. I knew that someone was approaching because Satchmo stood up from his resting position beside me. He was my personal warning system. He didn't bark or growl, while still obeying the 'stay' command that I had given him before I closed my eyes.

Kipton was no more than 10 years old, but he was an old soul and certainly mature beyond his years. He extended his hand confidently as he told me his name and asked if I was Brewster. I shook his hand and told him I was indeed who he thought I was. I couldn't help but notice the firm grip, as his little hand was engulfed by mine. I was impressed by how articulate he was as he spoke with purpose. He was clearly on a mission. His mother was watching from across the park with their dog, a Catahoula Leopard Dog named Charger.

Kipton was succinct. He asked me, "How can I get Charger in and out of his crate without having to battle it out with him?"

I smiled and said, "Who wins most of the battles?" He indicated Charger, with a slow roll of his eyes and head toward his mom and his dog across the park. The frustrated look on his face told me that Charger was scoring more points in the Game of Canine than Kipton. I asked him for some details and he told me that sometimes

Charger would willingly go in or come out of his crate but other times it was a fight to get him to do so.

I asked, "How big a fight usually takes place? Does Charger growl, snap or nip when he resists?"

"Sometimes he whines at me but never bites or anything", Kipton said. I told him the whine was Charger's way of protesting that he doesn't want to go in or out. It was also Charger posturing with him as if to say, "You're not the boss of me." I asked him if he knew what I meant by that.

He grinned as he said, "My sister says that to me sometimes when I tell her what to do."

I also said that if Charger growled he was warning him, and then he should stop immediately and let his mom or dad take over. "Has he ever bitten anyone?" I asked. He slowly shook his head definitively back and forth, with a stern look on his face to indicate *no.*

At this point Kipton's mother and Charger arrived and she commented on the difference in temperature under the canopy of the shade tree. She introduced herself as Kelly and then apologized for Kipton waking me up. She said that he'd heard about me from his friend at school, whose grandfather had recently talked to me about their Chihuahua. I remembered the conversation with George as I put my hand out to introduce myself. I told her that I'd been resting and not asleep. Satchmo's 'happy feet' showed his excitement as he wanted to interact with Charger, who was also quite excited. I asked them how Charger got along with other dogs and they both said, "Great." I suggested that we let the dogs run around and play for only a short while because of the blistering heat. Kelly unleashed Charger as I gave Satchmo the OK to take off.

I asked if Charger was a Catahoula Leopard Dog; they can have multiple colors, many different looks and often have different colored eyes, like a Siberian Husky. Charger certainly fitted the description. Kelly said yes and that he was a Katrina rescue dog. "He came with the name Charger. We guessed it's because that breed of dog use their heads to butt wild boars while herding them. He sometimes uses his head to herd us around as well", she said. "My brother, Jacob, loves the name because he drives a Dodge Charger." I laughed. Forty years ago my brother, David, also drove a Charger.

I told Kelly and Kipton the basics to the Game of Canine, including the Golden Rule and green-ring leader-energy. To redirect the conversation back to Charger's crate issues, I asked Kelly if Charger had problems only with Kipton or with other members of the family, as well. She indicated that most were with Kipton, herself and Louise, her eight-year-old daughter.

"My husband, Arthur, has no issues with Charger", she said. "He is a big man and Charger is very respectful of him."

I explained that Charger's resistance when going in and out of his crate was his way of ranking himself within the pack. If he got his way and refused to come out of his crate, or go in, then he won some points in the Game of Canine. This put him higher on the Leader Ladder than whoever was handling him. The reason he didn't give

Arthur a hard time was because he respected his higher position in the pecking order.

"Understand that the hierarchy of the pack is the most important thing on a dog's mind", I said. "It's necessary for the three of you; Kipton, Kelly and Louise, to position yourselves higher on your individual Leader Ladders, from Charger's perspective."

"Who walks Charger the most?"

"My dad", said Kipton. I suggested that Kipton join his father when he walked the dog.

"The walk", I said, "is the most important activity that you can do with a dog because it builds trust and respect when it is done correctly."

Kipton mentioned that when his dad walked Charger he always walked calmly beside him and didn't pull. When the others walked him, he pulled constantly.

"My point exactly", I said. "If you join your dad on his walks, you can practice taking the leash so that your dad can assist you in keeping Charger in a heel position at your side. This will put Charger in a subordinate position to you, as he walks respectfully without pulling on the leash. One of the ways to tell a dog that you are the alpha is to lead the *hunt*, which is a walk to us but simulates the raw form of hunting to them."

"By regularly practicing walking, and putting Charger in and out of his crate with your dad nearby, you will be consistently posturing yourself higher on your Leader Ladder than Charger. Have your dad increase his distance away from you and Charger as you progress with walking him, as well as putting him in and out of his crate. Eventually you won't need your dad to be with you as the pack becomes realigned. Make sure you include Louise and your mom when working with Charger. The three of you need to establish your pack pecking order, showing him how strong leaders all of you can be."

I also told them that a leader must always have calm, strong, green-ring energy and must never take *no* for an answer. "He does not get angry or upset but constantly presents his calm leader-energy, just as your dad does."

At this time, I looked around for Satchmo and Charger, who were running ecstatically through the creek, no doubt cooling off naturally. I was OK with this as they were having fun without bothering anyone else at the park. I suggested that Kipton use some treats to give Charger even more incentive to obey his commands. I asked him to try putting a treat just inside the crate when he wanted Charger to enter or just outside when he wanted him to exit.

Kipton frowned: "We don't have any treats to give him."

I asked if they had any carrots in their house. "Sure", he said. Dogs often like carrots because they are flavorful along with being crunchy and moist. Of course, they are nutritious as well.

I said, "My guess is that with you implementing all of the ideas that we just talked about, it will be much easier getting Charger to enter or exit his crate. This will also encourage his respect and trust for you on walks. I'm sure that you will have awesome success to report to me in the next couple of weeks.

**Dog Whisperer Story; animal hospitals**

I periodically give clinics at animal hospitals. Veterinarians and their staff are veterans at handling dogs. My objective is to add to their knowledge and help improve their effectiveness, by focusing on how dogs *think*. Their focus and skill set include knowing how dogs function and the physiology of a dog (rather than the *psychology*). I almost always focus on the most important thought on a dog's mind – ranking or pecking order. By understanding and respecting the significance of posturing and ranking to every dog, hospital staff can handle dogs even more competently.

When giving a clinic, I like to arrive early, to watch the staff deal with dogs. When a client and dog arrive, the receptionist commonly greets the dog in a high-pitched baby-talk voice while using a normal voice to greet the owner. When a dog and owner are received in this manner the dog perceives this as weakness, while the owner welcomes the friendliness. In this case it is not what you say but, more importantly, what you don't say (by not talking).

When I talk to the group about how they presently receive dogs into their clinic, I repeat what I've witnessed by acting it out using a whiny voice, exaggerating for effect. I then play the part of the receptionist *my* way, using calm, strong, green-ring energy. I approach the dog owner with a handshake as I introduce myself. I make solid eye contact with the owner and delay making eye contact with the dog. This is natural, or frontward, to a dog.

Next, I position myself with the dog either to my side or my back. If I am unsure or don't know the dog, I keep her within my peripheral vision, from the side. Otherwise I turn my back to the dog. This would be rude or backward to humans, but natural or frontward to dogs. What we consider snobby and rude, i.e., turning our back on someone and not acknowledging them, is a sign of strength and positive posturing to canines. Not paying attention to the dog strongly postures me in a dominant position, versus paying homage to him and positioning myself at a subservient level. We can't think like humans and feel that we are being rude if we ignore dogs.

When staff at animal hospitals begin their greetings by strongly posturing themselves, the whole visit will transpire much more smoothly. This includes both staff and vets. The dog will sense each person's calm, strong, leader-energy when not making eye contact immediately. As each staff member handles the dog and repeats this process, the dog will remain in a subordinate position. This very short investment of time will ensure that the dog's visit to the animal hospital will be much more pleasant for both humans and dogs; not necessarily perfect, but improved.

Once I complete my teachings about canine thinking, I always ask the staff, "Did you bring in some nasty, misbehaving dogs as I asked you to?" At every animal hospital, staff all answer this question identically. They roll their eyes wide and smirk, "Oh yeah, we have one of the worst dogs in our practice in a kennel for you." Their smug expression tells me they have no confidence in my ability to handle their difficult dog. I absolutely love it when I am underestimated, because the impact is so much greater when they witness me controlling *the calm,* with the dog respectful and friendly.

At this point they visualize the battle they typically encounter, accompanied by their fear of getting bitten, every time this misunderstood dog comes to the clinic. I, on the other hand, can only visualize the respectful behavior that I expect from all dogs. *If we can imagine it, we can achieve it.* As my mother (a special lady, to say the least) used to say, "Bruce – name it, then claim it. Imagine it first, and then make it happen." She instilled confidence in me that I continue to praise her for.

I then ask the staff to gather in the room with the dogs in kennels or crates, including the so called nasty beast, to show them how to move difficult dogs in and out of kennels or crates with ease. This is predicated on the exact same formula as when they welcome dogs at the front door. My first action is to stand in front of the kennel with my back to the dog. There is no risk of her hurting me from behind the kennel door. I then talk to the staff and reiterate the most important thought on the dog's mind; posturing or ranking or pecking order. I also tell them that by being humanly snobby, with my back to the dog and not making eye contact, I send my calm, strong energy as I posture with the dog. Typically, the dog will start to settle down as I communicate with them.

Next, I turn sideways with a peripheral view. The dog must be calm for me to turn frontward and make eye contact. It is never a good idea to make eye contact with an aggressive, strange dog, too soon. They consider this to be a challenge or a threat. Next, I stand in front of the kennel. The dog has ample time to read my green-ring energy. Then I put my foot in front of the kennel door and open it a little. If she pushes on the door to get out, my foot stops this from happening. She must remain calm for me to proceed.

Next, I partially open the door and quickly close it again. If she remains calm and does not lunge at the door, I open it wide and move forward to stand in her space and block her from exiting the kennel. These actions on my part are distinctive communications with her, using body language along with my alpha-energy, which she innately understands. At this time, I leash her and have her calmly exit the kennel because she is in a balanced mode, which is the key to facilitate success. She respects that I am 100 percent leader and therefore, she is 100 percent follower.

At this point it is *my* turn to be a little smug and have some fun. I turn to the staff, which usually are a little stunned, and say, "Is this the nasty beast you brought in for me? You said she was vicious. I say she is simply misunderstood." This usually gets a laugh. When they see the theory put into practice, they are suddenly believers in what I teach.

Next, I have the staff practice the process themselves with the so-called nasty dog, along with various other dogs within the hospital. This practice session proves invaluable in helping the staff develop their new skill set.

When a dog visits a vet, the allotted time to process them is usually about twenty minutes; the turnaround time from their arrival to the time they leave. By investing a minute or two to balance each dog, the remaining eighteen minutes can be calmly controlled and somewhat uneventful. A balanced dog, in the follower mode, is a happy dog, making her a pleasure to deal with. This balancing process should be initiated as soon as the dog and owner walk through the front door by whoever greets them. Each person who handles the dog must follow suit and continue the balancing process.

When the vet is finally introduced to the dog, he or she should wait a short period without making eye contact, exude green-ring energy and then step into their space. Everyone must consistently be calm and strong for this process to be effective. If the vet tech is nervous, the dog will know this, and respect is less likely to be established, often causing the dog to exert her dominance and possibly growl, nip or bite. Each person who handles the dog must individually align themselves with her. If their posturing is strong, they will be able to override a previous person's insecure or nervous energy. Dogs react to whatever is presented to them – they live in the moment.

**Summary**

The process of removing a dog from her crate at an animal hospital is identical to taking a dog out of her crate at home. Start with the right approach. Be indifferent to her while sending your green-ring energy. A dog should always be in a calm mode when exiting a crate. When you arrive home and want to let your dog out of her crate, invest a short minute to achieve a calm dog. When she calmly exits her crate, you are free to reward her with praise, play, treats or any other activity. An important rule in the Game of Canine is; When arriving home, ignore your dog until she shows you sixty seconds of respect, whether she's in a crate or not (see No. 5 in Chapter 31; "Six Ways to Say; I'm The Leader, Not You").

The reverse process, i.e., putting a dog in her crate, is essentially the same. You must start the process with calm energy. When a dog has issues with going into her crate, I suggest that you sit on the floor in front of the crate with her and give her a rub or maybe play with her. Incorporate some treats in this process to enhance the positive experience. The next move is to give her a treat with your hand a short distance into the crate. Give her lots of praise as she takes it. As she becomes comfortable with the process, toss a treat a short distance into the crate, forcing her to step inside. Let her out immediately and repeat this process while increasing the distance the treat is tossed into the crate. When she comfortably enters the crate, stop her from exiting for only a few seconds. Give lots of praise and rewards when she comes out.

You don't have to accomplish this process in one session. If she shows signs of reluctance, stop and try this again at another time. Eventually she will go in for her treat without much ado. This is a good time to block her from exiting the crate and make her wait for a short time, maybe thirty seconds. Keep increasing the time she stays inside. Progress to closing the door for about ten seconds and increase this to several minutes.

Next, walk away for a short time with the door closed and continue to extend this period that she's inside. Don't forget to praise and reward her when going in or out. This positive, progressive process will help her to enjoy her crate and likely wander in and out on her own, indicating total success. You can repeatedly practice this process well before you want to put her in her crate for a longer period.

## Chapter 29

## Six Ways to Say; "I'm the Leader, Not You."

*The alpha role is unique.*

I was exhausted one morning at the dog park because of a poor night's sleep. A neighbour's dog started barking incessantly at 3:30 a.m. and I never did get back to sleep. I silently called the neighbour many names; inconsiderate, disrespectful and narcissistic are the only ones that I can put in print. With my thick head and lack of energy, I was lucky the park was empty, and that I didn't have any major jobs to complete. My only obligation was to clean the park of dog waste, which is a main chore every Sunday morning.

As I mindlessly wandered about with my shovel and bucket, I became aware of a car that had pulled into the parking lot. I watched a very slight, young man leash his rambunctious Brittany Spaniel and immediately thought about the breed's endless energy, paired with their ultra-friendly nature. I can't think of a single negative associated with this breed. They make first-rate family pets, provided they get enough exercise. This sounds easy, but most people underestimate their extreme level of energy. I would classify them as extra high on the energy scale. A Bulldog would likely watch a Brittany tearing around and wonder what kind of drugs she was on?

My next thought was that if she was OK to play with Satchmo, he was in for a major workout. I smiled as I looked over to Satchmo and quietly said, "Hey." He looked at me, then back to the Brittany

Spaniel. Two great things about leash-free dog parks; dogs get to socialize with other dogs and they get lots of exercise.

I tried not to stare as I observed them walk across the parking lot and approach the entrance gate. The dog was pulling on the leash with such force that her owner was forced to quick-step along behind her. That's a lot of pulling for a forty-pound dog. The man was having trouble keeping his balance as she pulled him through the first and then the second gate. Already I was thinking about how this dog was leading the hunt (or walk), first through the parking lot and then through two gates. Both actions emphatically said to the Brittany, "You are the leader, not me."

Immediately upon entering the park the man tried to let his dog off the leash, but without much success. The dog was pulling so strongly that she was standing up on her hind legs and wiggling with unharnessed excitement. As soon as she was free, she launched herself like she'd stolen something and was making a getaway. Satchmo began whining because he wanted to run with her. The park was so quiet, I gave Satchmo the OK and off he went. As he approached the Brittany, they both stopped for a few seconds to size up each other's energy and then took off with glee.

We were the only humans in the park, so I moseyed over toward the young man and introduced myself. He told me that his name was Cooper and then said, "I've heard about you. You're the dog whisperer, aren't you?" I nodded affirmatively.

We watched our dogs as they frolicked through the creek, climbed the hill and back to the creek. Clearly, they were both in heaven. I told him Satchmo's name, and he told me his dog was Lizzie, named after his great-grandmother in England (officially Elizabeth, shortened to Lizzie). "The name is apropos because my gran was also very energetic. Even in her 90s she lived alone."

I asked if Lizzie ever ran out of gas and succumbed to fatigue.

"Not once", he answered. "She can go forever."

"This will be a stretch for Satchmo", I said. "He will push himself to keep up with her."

In football terms, Satchmo is built like a linebacker, muscular and quick, while Lizzy is like a wide receiver, lithe and fast with reams of endurance.

I asked Cooper what Lizzie was like if she didn't get her daily exercise. He responded with a resounding, "A pain in the butt. I notice the difference after even one day without a run. If I am sick and don't get her out for several days, she is unbearable. She whines, barks even more than usual, and is totally indifferent to anything I say. Even when she is exercised, I can't control her or stop her barking out the front window or in the yard. I love her a lot, in fact she is my best friend, but she is extremely demanding."

I mentioned Lizzie's pulling behavior while crossing the parking lot and through the gates into the park. I asked Cooper his thoughts on Lizzie's pulling and barking. "It's the only thing that I hate about her", he said. "If I could stop her barking in the house and pulling while out on a walk, she would be the perfect dog."

I told him how we act can say to a dog, 'You are the leader of the pack, not me.' Conversely, through our actions, it is just as easy to say, 'I'm the leader, not you.' "Pulling in front is certainly dominant behavior, and barking at things outside when she is in the house is protective behavior. Priority No. 1 in a dog's mind is ranking within the pecking order and, actually, it would inherently please her if you were her alpha."

I suggested he focus on two specific ways to positively position himself as the alpha with Lizzie, because she was continuously and emphatically posturing. The first idea I mentioned was keeping Lizzie on a leash while in the house for a few days. This would give Cooper a lot more control of her barking. The second idea that I mentioned was to have Lizzie walk beside Cooper and not in front, which is distinctly the leader's position. "You must enforce this with some tough love – no hurting, just not taking *no* for an answer. The walk is the most important activity that you can do with your dog. Maybe you should consider using a prong collar. It will be a game-changer for you."

Cooper said that he had a prong collar because a dog trainer had previously recommended it. The pet store had also suggested one. He added, "In the past whenever I have used it, the pulling was almost nonexistent. I don't like using it because I'm afraid it might hurt Lizzie. She's not a big 'muscle' dog that some people use them on."

I described how prong collars work without causing any pain, because the prongs aren't pointed. "The collar is designed to simulate an acute nip in the neck area. I suggest you give it another try. If fitted properly, it is a very effective tool in specific situations. It should fit snuggly, not too tight and not too loose. Be sure that you can easily get one finger under the prongs for a proper fit. Only a gentle correction with a wiggle of the leash should be necessary to keep her beside you while walking."

"By implementing these two things; keeping her leash on for a few days and re-introducing a prong collar; you will be changing the conversation with Lizzie – that you are the leader of your pack, not her."

Cooper said, "It can't hurt. I need to get better control of her. I didn't realize how important my behavior is. So, I can either say to her that she is the leader or that I am the leader, by my actions?"

"Exactly."

He laughed. "Sounds simple, I can't wait to give it a try. Are you here next Sunday?"

"You bet, I look forward to hearing how you make out. I know you will experience a major change in her behavior, resulting in you both being much happier. Remember, 'less is best', see how lightly you can flick the leash."

By this time Satchmo and Lizzie were cooling themselves by lying in the creek, panting frantically, with tongues hanging out the side of their mouths. We called our spent dogs and bid each other adieu. I went home shortly after Cooper left. I too was spent. As I drove home I thought about Cooper and Lizzie and decided that if they showed up next Sunday, I would give him a few more ways to say, "Lizzie, I'm the leader of this pack, not you."

## Dog Whisperer Lesson; speak canine, act like an alpha/leader

A major mistake that many dog owners make is to say to their dogs, “You are the leader of the pack, not me.” This forces a dog to assume the highest pack position, and to dominate and protect the pack becomes their mission, resulting in misbehavior. We don’t say this in words; we say this by our actions. Typically, we don’t even know that we’ve said it. The objective here is to teach you how to say, “I’m the leader of the pack, not you.” This will have an enormous impact in the turnaround of negative behavior to positive behavior.

Earlier in the book (Chapter 19; The Combo-Pack; Humans and Dogs), there is a list of both dominant and protective behaviors. The goal is to have a balanced pack with the dog thinking that he is at the bottom of the hierarchy and their owner is at the top. It can make the difference between feeling proud or embarrassed, calm or angry, pleased or frustrated. Both humans and canines revel in a clearly balanced hierarchy.

There are six different ways to distinctly say to our dogs, “I’m the leader”, versus “You are the leader.” The establishment of position is innately important to the canine nature. It involves a pure system consisting of only leaders or followers, with no role changes.

**Six ways to say; “I’m the leader, not you.”**

The following six behaviors will send a message to a dog in their language. We automatically do all six behaviors from the human point of view (natural or frontward to us and unnatural or backward to them), therefore giving a negative message. By turning things around and reversing the order (unnatural or backward to us and natural or frontward to our dogs), the message suddenly becomes a positive one. All six behaviors are instinctive and implicitly important to dogs; there is no priority to the listings.

1. **"I lead the hunt."**

The hunt to a dog is a walk to us. Therefore, it is you, the human, who must lead the walk. In the wild, no member of the pack passes the leader, unless he directs a low-ranking pack member to lead as a *tester* to see if it is safe ahead; this saves the pack from putting the valuable bloodline of the breeding male and female at risk. Other than that, if the alpha allowed a pack member to take the lead, it would mean that he'd relinquished the leader position to that pack member. It would also mean that he would be kicked out of the pack and become a lone wolf looking for another pack to integrate into. This is how serious the lead position is on a hunt/walk.

When a dog pulls on the leash to be out in front, he is showing dominance. You must reverse this and lead the hunt yourself. As he tries to get in front of you, quickly change directions so he must react and catch up to you. If you are able, you can even run in the new direction. As soon as he catches up to you, change direction again. Repeat this several times to force him to keep his attention on you. Also, keep changing speeds as you walk, from fast to slow to normal. You could also give the leash a pop to the side, which will unbalance him a little and direct his focus to you. When you pop him sideways, be sure that the leash is parallel to the ground, which will maximize the effect of your sideways pop. If he is persistent then you too must be persistent, but even more so. You must win this battle. If you get angry or upset, your negative energy will be perceived as a weakness. Be patient. Play his game, his way. Remember that dog-time is slower than human-time.

Normally this behavior is remarkably easy to overcome. The dog likely doesn't really want the out-front dominant position in the first place.

By consistently saying, "I am the leader, not you", by leading the hunt, your dog will respectfully walk beside you in the heel position, like being in an imaginary box. The box needs to be proportionate to the size of the dog. Obviously, a Chihuahua's box will be the size of a shoebox, while a Great Dane's will be the size of a refrigerator. I am a huge proponent of praising positive behavior and interrupting negative behavior. This way a dog knows exactly what behavior you like and dislike.

*The walk, or hunt, is the most important activity that you can do with your dog. It builds trust and respect.* They trust that you will not lead them into harm's way, while respectfully follow wherever you want to go. To have a dog respectfully walk beside you will fill you with pride. You will stand out like a sore thumb, because very few dog owners achieve this result. I am dazzled when dogs known as *pullers* walk perfectly beside their owners when we go outside. I love it when I jokingly get to say to an owner, "I thought your dog was a puller." Their usual response is, "I can't believe this is my dog."

My usual response is, "You now have the key to unleashing your dog's potential, while maintaining a balanced pack. Diligently play by the rules to the Game of Canine."

I once worked with a couple of farm dogs that had never in their lives been on a leash. They were both Hungarian Kuvasz's, whose job was to guard a herd of sheep. A Kuvasz looks like a Great Pyrenees (big, white and hairy), designed to simulate the look of a sheep and blend into the herd. I was called because they were starting to show aggression toward the farm workers. They lived outside with the sheep, either in the sheep's paddock or out in the field. Whenever the vet was needed, he would come to the farm to check out both the sheep and dogs, and hence they never left the farm, nor were they ever leashed.

When we went for a walk down the laneway, while leashed, they walked ideally beside me, showing tremendous respect. Every time I stopped, they stopped and sat, with absolutely no training. The farmer was amazed that his dogs knew how to do this. This behavior is inherent, (canine DNA), i.e., to respectfully not pass the leader. Their dominant aggression dissipated, as well. It was at this point the farmer told me that his dogs had never been leashed or in the house before that day.

2. **"I go in and out of doors first."**

When the pack leaves or returns to their den, the leader always goes out or in first. The reason is to make sure that there is no imminent danger either outside or inside the den. When leaving the den, he steps out and uses his ultra-perceptive radar system to sense for any danger. Utilizing his other senses of smell, sight and hearing, he detects if it is safe or not. The same process is repeated when they return to the den. All pack members stop and wait for him to enter and make sure there are no bears, cougars or other bad guys in their den.

To accomplish this process when going in/out of doors with your dog, stop at the doorway, give a 'sit/stay' command with a hand signal and/or voice, then step in or out while he calmly waits a few seconds for your next command. Keep a close eye on your dog, otherwise he may disobey and proceed to move forward. Next, give him a 'come' command, using a hand signal and/or voice. He should calmly proceed through the doorway and stop to wait for you to close the door. Do not let him pass you and proceed to a forward dominant position. This will quickly become automatic. It's part of their DNA for the leader to go in and out first.

3. **"I eat first."**

The leader always eats first in the canine pack. He must keep strong so that he can roam his territory to find food, along with protecting his pack. If the pack kills a small animal, say a rabbit, the leader eats the whole thing himself, leaving nothing for the others. If their kill is a large animal, all pack members wait until the leader finishes eating before they eat.

To emphasize this fact, you must *fake* eating their dog food before they eat, specifically when they are about to put their snouts into their food bowl. Obviously, you are not about to eat dog-food, so the key word is *fake*.

Feeding should take sixty seconds, encompassing three twenty second segments. In the first twenty seconds *scent* the food. I suggest that you run your hands through the food for these twenty seconds. If you feed your dog wet food and you don't want to get your hands yucky, just rub your palm in a circle around the top of the food to leave your scent. If you feed raw food this 20 second segment could be eliminated. I take Satchmo's dry food from a large pail by hand. I put seven handfuls into his bowl, while continuously running it through my hand.

The second twenty second segment is to *fake* eating the food and *spit* into his food. To do this, your dog should be with you waiting to be fed. While feeding Satchmo I hold the bowl up high to my face and make some noise, indicating that I am eating. I could also turn my back on him. I slurp and munch to fake the process. At the same time, I continue to run the top portion of the food through my hand to accentuate the scenting process. To increase the impact, I spit in his food several times at the end of the twenty seconds. This may sound gross to some, but the intent is for him to also smell my saliva. I have a little sip of water to swish around in my mouth before I feed him.

In the third twenty second interval, put the food on the floor and make him *wait* for twenty seconds. This distinctly postures you in the leader's position while he remains in a subservient position as he waits. This is a good opportunity for some obedience training, utilizing a 'sit/stay' command. I wash my hands during this time before I give Satchmo the OK to eat.

Many people find this the most impactful way to say, "I am the leader, not you." Often dogs will drool profusely during the whole process.

A client once told me about feeding her dog when her cottage was full of guests. Because she felt embarrassed about spitting in her dog's food at feeding time, she omitted this in front of her guests. Her dog smelled the food before he was about to eat and then walked across the kitchen and just looked at the food bowl. Three separate times he approached the food for another smell but didn't eat. My client decided that she'd needed to have a sip of water and spit in his food as usual. Her dog approached the food, had a smell and was finally content to eat once he smelled his leader's scent of saliva, indicating that she had eaten first. This was a natural display of respect.

If your dog is a grazer and eats sporadically throughout the day, he is not recognizing or respecting the fact that you provided his food. This is dominant behavior. My recommendation is to feed your dog using the three 20-second intervals mentioned above. I would allow about 10 minutes for him to eat, and if he has not shown much interest I would then pick up his food bowl and wait until the next feeding time. Keep repeating this procedure until he gets the idea that he must eat when the food is provided by you. The choice to eat, or not, is *his*; the food is available. Don't fret; he won't starve if he goes without eating for a day or more. It shouldn't take long for him to catch on to the new feeding process. His hunger will prevail.

4. **"I control the door."**

When a pack of wolves is resting in their den, they have a sentry at all openings. The purpose of this sentry is to quietly warn the leader if they sense any danger outside. They do not bark at whatever they sense because this would broadcast their location. The leader steps in front of the sentry and assesses the situation himself. His options are; freeze, fight or flight. He can order the pack to freeze and not make a sound, as the potential intruder passes by without detecting the pack; he can attack the potential intruder because it's a threat or their next meal; or he can instruct the pack to flee from the intruder if it presents a risk. The bottom line is that it is the leader's job to make these executive decisions; not a pack member's.

In the combo-pack of canines and humans, the same rule exists. It is the leader's job to control the door and make decisions regarding this area. There are two positions to take control of when visitors arrive at the door; from *afar* and from *near*.

**From afar**

When you are expecting guests, proactive management is to leash your dog well before their expected time of arrival. When someone either knocks or rings the doorbell, your dog's normal expected response is likely to bark and run to the door. Because you have him leashed, you have control, from afar, of the door. The mandate is to calm your dog before you move from wherever you are in the home when the guest rings. Next, you want to proceed toward the door while maintaining a calm dog. You may need to stop multiple times on route to the door, to re-calm him, if he gets rambunctious.

Stop about eight feet before the door and give a 'sit/stay' command. You are now prepared to answer the door.

**From near**

When someone knocks or rings the doorbell unexpectedly, dogs often run to the door, barking incessantly. Your mandate is to *control the calm* at the door. If your dog is barking or overly exuberant, step in front of him, putting your back to the door and facing your dog. Interrupt him with a sharp 'Hey' sound and/or a clap. Step into his space/face, and then take his space by shooing or shuffling him backward. You should have a certain spot that is used every time someone comes to the door; about eight feet back from the door. Next, leash him and get him calm. This may take a bit of effort. You can always yell out to the visitor, "I'll be right there, I have to control my dog(s)." They will assuredly get the picture, thanks to the intensive barking. Next, give a 'sit/stay' command and prepare to answer the door.

The process of controlling the door from near or afar is the same from this point forward. The eight-foot spot from the door will become his special place to calmly wait every time someone visits. Focus on not giving up control. If you turn your back to him as you face the door, you will quickly lose control because you will have no idea what he is doing. He could easily run past you before you realize it. By standing sideways to keep a peripheral view, a quick turn of your head will give you an instant connection to both your dog and guest. You can easily talk to your visitors while keeping an eye on the dog. If he starts to get excited, interrupt him to regain a calm dog. If need be, step into his space and give a light correctional pop on the leash. With authority, repeat the 'sit/stay' command. With some practice (organize family members or friends to knock on your door), he will quickly learn to remain calm in his sit/stay position while you answer the door.

This is a huge hurdle to overcome for so many dog owners. By mastering door control, answering the door with your dog will become a pleasure that will make you proud. This is where diligently practicing many short obedience training sessions of one, two or three commands; (come, sit and stay) will pay off in a big way. Don't forget to praise and/or treat him.

5. **"I ignore him when coming home."**

The only member of the canine pack to leave the pack on his own, is the leader. No other members leave the pack by themselves. The pack does everything together and the power of the pack is daunting. The reasons the leader leaves are to check out his territory: to discover where to lead his pack on a hunt; if other wolves are marking in his territory; to find a water source; to find new living quarters; or anything else that would affect his pack. When the canine alpha returns to his pack, he calmly goes to his throne area. This is notably the highest position in the den area. He then waits for his pack to settle down and show him respect. This show of respect is what we must simulate when returning home to our dogs. (This is the same process that takes place in the military. If a general enters a room full of subordinates, they immediately stand and salute the general in a show of respect.)

Typically, when arriving home, we like to give our dogs an excited hello and make a big deal of seeing them. We like being welcomed by an excited, loving dog. After enjoying a short period of excitement, things settle down and go calm. This is natural or frontward to humans but unnatural or backward to canines. We must reverse this process. For them to be calm when we arrive home, they must show us respect for a short period and then excitement after that.

I suggest that when returning home, you ignore your four-legged family member until they give you about sixty seconds of respect. This means that you don't acknowledge their presence in any way. No talking, no eye contact, no petting them – absolutely no connecting with them whatsoever, until they give you, their leader, the respect that is deserved.

When entering your home, if you are accosted by your dog, albeit in a friendly way, he is saying to you, "Hey you, pay homage to me. I want attention because I am higher on the Leader Ladder than you. It's all about me, me, me." We typically contribute to this mindset because we engage them in an excited manner. However, this leads to imbalance within your pack. Therefore, it is mandatory for you to establish a higher position in the pecking order by ignoring them until they show subservience and respect to you.

This is where, *control the calm to win the game,* comes into play. If they will not settle and you have had enough of their persistent exuberance and demands for your attention, I suggest that you interrupt them with a blast of energy. This can be accomplished by simultaneously giving a dynamic, very loud and sharp 'Hey' sound, accompanied with a big clapping sound. Next, immediately turn and walk away from them. They will likely be shocked and disconnected from you at this point and will have to start posturing with you all over again, to try and establish their dominance. Repeat this if needed until they show you respect via a *calm*.

When they show respect for approximately sixty seconds by calmly standing, sitting or lying, then crank up the pandemonium with hugs, praise, play, and give them all the love you want – on your terms. Always praise positive and interrupt negative behavior.

6. **"I live higher than you."**

In the canine world, the pack hierarchy can be determined by height. If there is a pack of ten canines lying on the grass, we could not identify the hierarchy within the pack, but each pack member would distinctly know the pecking order. They could be wolves, dingoes, feral dogs, coyotes, domestic dogs or any other canine. If they were moved onto a set of stairs to rest, they would arrange themselves in order according to the height of each step. The leader would be on the top step, and all others would position themselves in a descending order down the stairs, with the omega, the lowest pack member, on the bottom step. It is remarkable how this works. Their pack pecking order, or hierarchy, would be unmistakably displayed to us by the position of each step.

I witnessed this at a doggie-day-care one afternoon just prior to giving the staff a clinic. They had about six different fenced-off areas or paddocks, each with compatible dogs within it. When I went into a paddock where about six dogs were resting, I noticed a dog lying on the top of the doghouse, the highest position in the paddock. Next, I noticed a dog on the picnic table, the second highest position; and then a third lying on the bench of the table. The descending order continued: there was another on a small berm of dirt; another on the sidewalk and the last one, the omega, was lying on the lowest point, on the grass next to the gate. This display of pack posture was evident by their position in terms of height.

I asked the women who ran the day care about the pecking order in this paddock. They both pointed to the Border Collie positioned on the berm. I mentioned the dog that I believed to be the alpha. They asked how I knew this and I said, "Because of their posturing by height." I proceeded to show them the descending pack order; leader on top of the doghouse, next on the picnic table, next on the bench, etc. I continued to outline the order down to the omega on the grass. I also mentioned that the answer to my question about the hierarchy within the paddock area should have indicated that the human was on top. From their guests' point of view, the humans must always be perceived as the alpha. This situation was the starting point of my presentation to the day-care staff.

Based on this foundation of pack posturing, whenever a dog comes up onto your bed or couch, they are suddenly at the leader's level of height. Often a small dog will sit on top of the back of the couch or want to climb onto your shoulder or even the top of your head. From their mindset the higher the better. Many dogs will sit on stairs or on the top of the couch, to look out the front window. These are distinctive positions of being on-duty in a protective mode. When I am teaching this concept to people with unbalanced dogs, I suggest that they don't let their dog on the bed or couch for a short period of time, say, a couple of weeks. This will send a direct message to the canine that their alpha is perched on the highest level.

The usual question that I'm asked at this point is, "How do I keep him off the bed in the middle of the night?" My answer is, "Introduce him to Niagara Falls." By gently nudging him toward the edge of the bed, whether it is the middle of the night or first thing in the morning, he gets sent 'over the falls'. This will not hurt him in any way. Just keep nudging him until he goes over the edge. As soon as you hear his feet hit the floor, it's all over. No anger or saying a single word; just introduce him to Niagara Falls. Within one or two nights he will remain on the floor, as no one wants to get sent over the falls when they are sound asleep.

The process is the same for a couch. When you're sitting on a chair or couch, be proactive and interrupt him before he makes his move to jump up beside you. If you're not ready for him and he jumps up, just give him the nudge until he goes over the falls. If you catch him on the couch, approach him with an interrupting sound of 'Hey' or a clap and nudge him off. Often this is all it takes. He already knows the height rule. If he gives you a hard time by growling or snarling, use a pillow to push him off. The pillow will protect you as he gets sent over the falls. You can also create the scenario and set him up by leashing him and leave the room until he gets back up on the couch. Having the leash already on him will give you significant more control. The bottom line is that he must go over the edge to the floor.

A couple of weeks after the pack has been rebalanced, I suggest that the only time your dog comes up onto either the bed or couch is when you invite him up. At this point it is a good idea to pick one or the other. In other words, he is never allowed on the bed again and can only get on the couch when invited, or vice versa. This will give you some solid control or positioning of height. Remember, the leader always takes the highest position, so be cognizant of living higher than your dog.

Regarding the above six rules; every time we break one of these rules, we send a very distinct message to our dog; "You are the leader of the pack, not me." Confusion about pack hierarchy is the No.1 cause of canine misbehavior. Inconsistent leadership creates anarchy as a dog wrestles us for position. I call this a *self-inflicted curse*. The key to changing negative behavior to positive behavior is to play by the rules to the Game of Canine as closely as possible. Follow The Recipe. This will unleash your dog's full potential, so he can become the special balanced dog that every dog owner wants.

**Summary**

A big component of understanding the canine way is knowing their modes of communication. Canines never use words to converse. They use a plethora of physical actions to broadcast their messages. Dog owners frequently give the wrong message to their dogs because they don't know how to communicate in the language of canine. Like most things, it is easy once it is revealed. How often have we all said something that we wish we hadn't? Sometimes it's not a big deal, while other times it creates embarrassment and serious problems. The very same can be said when communicating with dogs. My focus is on the negative message that we don't even know we're sending. It is the accumulative effect of repeating things that we would not likely 'say' if we were cognizant of what we are saying. Dog owners habitually make the mistake of saying to their dog, "You are the leader-of-the-pack, not me." That said, we can just as matter-of-factly send a message to a dog, through our actions, to take the follower's position by saying, "I'm the leader of the pack, not you."

By utilizing the above six ways to say to your dog, "I am the leader of the pack, not you", major problems can be avoided. If problem behavior has already developed, by consistently changing the message regarding leadership, you can help your dog assume a subordinate follower position. This will result in balance within your pack, along with positive behavior. I cannot stress enough the importance of saying exactly what you really mean, and meaning exactly what you say. Eliminate confusing messages by learning how to clearly communicate in the language of canine. Focus on utilizing all six ways to say, "I am the leader of this pack, not you."

# Conclusion

## *The Game of Canine*

## Basics

***Black or White versus Gray:* My biggest hurdle when teaching dog psychology is getting gray humans to act black or white canine; either you lead, or the dog must. This is not complex or difficult to understand. A child can follow the rules; but it is unnatural for us to act black or white. Our DNA is gray, or loose. Humans must therefore focus on and practice these new rules to achieve and maintain a balanced pack forever.**

Control the calm to win the game.

Posturing; Ranking; Hierarchy; Pecking Order – These are all synonyms in the Game of Canine. This is a canine's most important thought. Their posturing with us never stops.

Leader's job: Dominate and protect the pack.

Follower's job: Respect, obey and serve the leader.

My favorite question, "When did I give up control?"
The answer must be, "I didn't."

Daily obedience: 25 commands per day; Come, Sit, Stay, Down, Heel.

25 calms per day: Three ways to get a calm:

1. Calmly go in/out an outside door.
2. Change an excited dog back to calm, within five seconds.
3. They respectfully give you a calm when doing things that used to get them excited (in a negative fashion).

Note: 25 commands and calms per day, total 175 of each per week, and 700 per month. Establishing this, will rank you at the top of your Leader Ladder.

## 18 Rules in "The Game of Canine"

**Note: An asterisk (*) indicates the two most important rules of the game. Master these and you are poised to win the game.**

### The Golden Rule

*** 1. Tell them once and *never* take *no* for an answer.**
***("It's an order 'private canine'.")***

### Five Ways To Communicate

*** 2. Energy: Focus on calm, strong, green-ring, leader-energy.**

3. Body Language: Use these cues: Stare; Put your hand above their head; Step into their face/space; Take their space; Squeeze their neck; Pinch their scruff; Put your hand over their snout.
4. A Loose Leash exudes leader-energy.
5. Use Hand Signals for: Come, Sit, Stay, Down, Heel.
6. Words: Try using no words for a week; weird but effective.

The objective is to eliminate the 'chit chat' and focus on using the first four, far more effective ways, to communicate.

### Six Ways To Interrupt Negative Behavior

7. Say "Hey".
8. Clap your hands.
9. Pop or flick the leash. (Don't pull.)
10. Poke their neck or belly to simulate a bite.
11. Put your hand on their throat to simulate a kill bite.
12. Grab the scruff of their neck; Lift their front feet off the ground or push them to the ground. **Only** use this if they are insubordinate or show aggression.

## Six Ways To Say; "I'm The Leader, Not You."

13. I lead the hunt/walk.
14. I go in and out of doors first.
15. I eat first: 20 seconds scent their food; 20 seconds fake eating and spit; 20 seconds wait, with food on the floor.
16. I control the door with visitors; from afar and near.
17. I ignore them when I come home, until they give me 60 seconds of respect.
18. I live higher than them; no bed or couch for them.

**Good luck.**

**Climb your Leader Ladder and become their General.**

**www.canadiandogwhisperer.ca**